AMERICAN ARCHITECTURE
a vintage postcard collection

AMERICAN ARCHITECTURE
a vintage postcard collection

Luc Van Malderen
Foreword by Cesar Pelli

FUTURE NEW YORK
A 1911 science-fiction drawing by Pettit & Richard Rummell. Published on the front cover of the 1926 and 1928 Album "King's Views of New York" (Edition Manhattan Postcards Co).
Many similar postcards exist. At first "dirigable airships" were portrayed in the sky before being replaced by "future aeroplanes".
Several buildings can be distinguished on the postcard and distinctly, on the left, the Singer Tower and in the centre, the New York Municipal Building.

Future New York, "The City of Skyscrapers," New York.

First published in Australia in 2000 by
The Images Publishing Group Pty Ltd
ACN 059 734 431
6 Bastow Place, Mulgrave, Victoria, 3170
Telephone (61 3) 9561 5544 Facsimile (61 3) 9561 4860

Copyright © The Images Publishing Group Pty Ltd 2000

All rights reserved. Apart from any fair dealing
for the purposes of private study, research,
criticism or review as permitted under the Copyright Act,
no part of this publication may be reproduced,
stored in a retrieval system or transmitted in
any form by any means, electronic, mechanical,
photocopying, recording or otherwise, without the
written permission of the publisher.

National Library of Australia Cataloguing-in-Publication Data

Malderen, Luc Van, 1930–.
American architecture : a vintage postcard collection.

ISBN 1 86470 078 5

1. Postcards. 2. Architecture, American. 3. Architecture,
Modern – 20th century – United States. I. Title

720.923

Designed by The Graphic Image Studio Pty Ltd,
Mulgrave, Australia
Film by PrePress
Printed in Hong Kong

ACKNOWLEDGEMENTS

The author is deeply grateful to many people who have stimulated and given support, in ways known or unknown to them, and without in any way being responsible for the contents. Some friends offered precious postcards, others have lent support and quite a number have day after day (I have been collecting for 13 years now!) forwarded advice and help. I thank them all.

Sandrine ALOUF, director, Fondation pour l'Architecture - Brussels
Christine BASTIN and Jacques EVRARD, photographers - Brussels
Claire BORING TERLINDEN - Dallas
Gérome CORNETTE, Columbia University - New York
Marc CRUNELLE, architect - Brussels
Michel de CALUWE, Marketing Communication Director, Imperbel - Brussels
Gérard FINEL, editing consultant - Paris
Jean-Pierre HARDENNE and France VAN LAETHEM, architects - Montreal
Françoise and the late Peter KNEEBONE JOLLANT, designers - Paris
Pascal LEMAITRE, illustrator - New York
Marc LUMER, art director - Los Angeles
Pascale MALILO, graphic designer - Brussels
Marianne MARECHAL, artist - Brussels
Michel MICHIELS, director, Ad Corporate - Brussels
Caroline MIEROP, architect - Brussels
Catherine MILLER FASBENDER, Harvard University - Cambridge
Pauline PAIRON, fashion designer - Paris
Marcel PESLEUX, director, ISAE (La Cambre) - Brussels
Marina CHAUCHE PONJEART, designer - Paris
Pierre PUTTEMANS, architect - Brussels
Guy SCHOCKAERT, president, ICOGRADA - Brussels
Michel and Susan SOUTHWORTH, Harvard University - Cambridge
Robert TREVISIOL, architect - Brussels
Claudine VAN DEN ABEELE, artist - Brussels/Miami
Arlette ZUCOLI VERMEIREN, designer - Milano
and more distinguished friends and relations.

Anna LUBINSKA deserves special recognition for helping me with my somewhat doubtful English and translating the original French Introduction.

I should also mention the authors of specialized books and guides who have helped me all the way through. Eighty publications in all!

Finally the book would not exist without the combined heedfulness of Jacqueline PAIRON, University of Louvain; Christian LASSERRE, president of CIAUD - Brussels; and Georges BINDER, managing director of Buildings & Data s.a. - Brussels. I owe them a debt of gratitude.

60 BOOK TOWER, 81 FLOORS, DETROIT, MICH.

Foreword

I have always enjoyed receiving postcards. They carry warm connotations of friendship. They are like a *hello* at a distance. The quality of the images is not critical. They are impressions to share among friends. Postcards have some of the iconic qualities of religious stamps. The latter are sacred symbols and the former are popular ones; but they both stand for something else more important, and they both carry, or try to carry, emotions in their message.

I enjoy also looking at postcards in their racks in shops and in collections at antique fairs. They tend to offer the most popular views, usually in the most obvious manner. They become poignant after time passes and many of the urban and natural landscapes they describe have sometimes changed radically. What was once a common everyday scene cannot be seen any more.

Postcards belong to the 20th century. They did not exist before and I doubt they will survive long in the 21st century when we already have other faster, more personal, ways of keeping in touch and sending images, over the wire or the ether. But, in the 20th century, they became and remain as key witnesses of the things we see and the way we see them.

I greatly enjoy discovering my buildings as subjects for postcards. They are a sort of proof that the structures I designed have resonated at a popular level. Whatever artistic value we may aspire to for our works, for architecture to have any meaning, must touch a popular chord. Buildings belong to their cities and their citizens and architecture is, above all, a social art.

Many of the images in the collection of postcards in this book have lost meaning for us today. Others are appealing because they represent cherished buildings that we have lost. But, I enjoy most those of our great skyscrapers, primarily the Chrysler and Empire State buildings. They were able somehow to respond to everyone's view of what a great tall building should be. Almost 70 years after their construction they are still wonderful, strong, proud pieces of architecture. They remain symbols of optimism and they suggest a bright new world. Postcards of them continue to be made, sold and sent carrying messages to all corners of the world.

Practically all of the images in this book belong to the past; in the subjects chosen, the way they were photographed and the techniques of colouring and reproducing them. They represent a selection of roughly the first three decades of our century and they are unlike contemporary postcards in many ways. This collection of images can also be seen as a collection of old visions and hopes, like dried flowers we could also have kept within the leaves of this same book.

Cesar Pelli

THE BOOK TOWER, Detroit, Michigan
The initial Building between the two towers was built in 1917 by arch. L. Kamper. The book Tower was constructed by the same architect in 1926, but the New Book Tower, that was to rise 873 feet in the air (81 floors) never existed. The 1929 financial crash put a stop to Mr. J.B. Book, Jr's dream to what was to be the tallest building in the world.

Introduction to a Collection of Architectural Postcards.

Fig. 1

1 COENTIES SLIP, New York City, New York
   Once Coenties Slip was one of the early city's largest wharves. The inlet has been completely filled in. At this point, the old Third Avenue El made a spectacular zigzag turn. Built in 1879 and dismantled in 1950. Collotype print.

2 EMPIRE STATE BUILDING, New York City, New York
   Architectural rendering of the Empire State Building.

3&4 GULF BUILDING, Houston, Texas
   A coloured night view made from a daytime postcard.

Saturday, May 12th, 1987. I had just finished a series of lectures at the University of Oregon, Eugene, and was enjoying a peaceful walk. I hit upon a junk shop: inside, on an old little table, I saw a green ceramic bowl with 12 postcards in it.

They were all from the 30s and were of Art Deco-style skyscrapers. Later, I was to discover the existence of Art Deco-style postcards of Neo-Classic and Revival buildings!

I bought the whole lot, and took them back gleefully to decorate the walls of my room.

Today, I have over six thousand postcards in my possession. Practically all of them are typical of American architecture and cover the turn of the century, up to 1935-40. A fine collection of vintage postcards.

In my view, there are two interesting points to these postcards. On the one hand, their unique and original graphic design, and on the other, American architecture in general. Both very big interests of mine.

Around 1900, they were either printed or lithographed in colour or typeset, whilst in Europe most postcards were produced in halftones and printed using the magnificent collotype technique which did not require dot-screening, but which took rather a long time to print (image 1). This was the reason why that particular technique died out.

The Americans - quite rightly too - have always been very proud of their architecture. Their high-rise buildings and skyscrapers that seem to surge out of the ground were famous even before they were completed, and sometimes the postcard was printed even before the official opening took place.

These postcards are not really rare, so they are not particularly expensive to buy. I have found them in the Benelux countries, France, Germany, England and, of course, in the States. But a postcard that you get from across the Atlantic is intrinsically precious, because it has travelled by rail and by ship. You're bound to keep it. Who would throw away a postcard from so far away! Nowadays such postcards are not only common souvenirs but also valuable reference documentation for museums, architectural foundations and researchers. The very technique used at the time enables one to understand the architecture better and works on architecture that make reference to postcards are countless.

Most of the postcards were drawn or redrawn from photographs. Goodbye to perspective and long live vertical lines that stay vertical. The initial document known as the skeleton (in black and white) was coloured in by chromists - a profession which disappeared 25 years ago. Very skilfully, they coloured in films and chose the amalgams (the mix of colours for printing) and textures of aleatory screens, flat colours. A far cry from ordinary realism - which is what makes them so delightful.

The result is sometimes very delicate and fine and sometimes quite clumsy, even primitive. All visual obstacles, even tall neighbours, were discarded and only the building - in all its unique glory - remained.

Then, you also have architectural renderings *à la* Hugh Ferris (1889 - 1962) (image 2) and night views which were in fact day views that had been coloured in (images 3 and 4). But how charming they are, and what imagination. Real works of art in fact. The sky was often one big flat blue colour or one big mass of clouds.

There are some buildings that are identical except for the fact that the sky colours are different with the customary halftone veering to a cyclamen rose or tangerine as it nears the horizon.

I have since discovered that this used to be one of the tricks of the primitive Flemish artists of the 16th century!

NEVER EXPECT MORE THAN YOU GET

Collecting is like hoarding, not a particularly dangerous pastime unless your hobby happens to be collecting bathtubs.

Thirteen years on, I know, for sure that I've covered the subject, but how many more interesting postcards are still out there, no-one can ever know.

There are some amazing buildings that have not been honoured with a postcard, and there are some miserable little postcards, that do not do honour to the subject they are supposed to portray, and that are not worth mentioning.

Then, there are those cards that turn up scratched, dog-eared, torn or faded, or where the colours have been printed off-centre. They are not included in my collection, but are not in the wastepaper basket, either ... yet.

Out of the 100 postcards selected on the basis of two important criteria - relevance and the beauty of their graphic rendering - there are 40 from New York, 20 from Chicago, and a total of 40 from other North American cities, in particular, Detroit, Philadelphia and San Francisco, and to a lesser degree Baltimore, Boston, Cleveland, Los Angeles, Pittsburgh, St. Louis and Washington. This ratio is surprisingly applicable on a global scale.

I have purposely not included irrelevant postcards portraying the great outdoors, tourist spots and sights, Indians or humourous little curiosities. On the other hand, I have included some remarkable bridges and beautifully drawn industrial plants ... and a few other postcards, just for fun.

One is sometimes tempted to read the message on the card. This is indiscreet and not worth the bother. You find out that the sea was a like a pond or absolutely foul; that one is on top form or just shattered; that it was really too hot or - alternatively - freezing, and then, that 'you absolutely must kiss so-and-so' who you really don't want to ... and all this in different languages of course.

Fig. 3

Fig. 4

DATES AND DATA

In the beginning, postcards were printed by the state. The May 19th 1898 Act of Congress enabled postcards to be printed privately. At the time, the domestic postal rate was one cent. In 1917 it was raised to two cents. On July 1st 1919 it was dropped back down to one cent until July 1st 1928, when it became two cents again!

The saga ended on August 1st 1958 when the rate shot up to three cents.

All this makes it difficult to date postcards accurately since at that time, in the United States, the year was not necessarily mentioned on the postmark and writers rarely date postcards (as well as sometimes being downright illegible!).

Today I can still mail a postcard that was printed way back in 1900, and it will reach its destination postmarked 2000!

On March 1st 1907, a federal law was passed allowing messages to be written on the back of postcards (in Europe it was law since 1904). Formerly, the space on the back was only used for the name and address (image 5). This is the reason why, initially small type plates were printed on the recto leaving space for writing around them (image 6).

Even though the habit of writing on the back came into practice, this did not really change people's habit of writing on the front as well (image 7).

To my knowledge, there is no official, or unofficial catalogue of vintage postcards in North America. An interesting detail: in the 1900s a great number of postcards were actually printed in Germany. But to conceal their origin, sometimes the phrase 'printed in Bavaria' was used instead!

It seems that such commercial practices came to an end around 1910, when Curt Teich set up a nationwide postcard business. Based in Chicago, he used to take the train and photograph cities along the track. A few days later, travellers would be offered the famous linen cards. However, looking at his company's plant (1898 - 1974) this could be partly legend (image 8). His company printed 360,000 different postcards in all.

LET'S TALK ARCHITECTURE

An introduction is perhaps not really the right place to talk about the history of architecture, but looking at the buildings and spectacular architectural style makes you notice things you may not have seen before.

Leaving popular architecture and immigrants' cute simple wooden houses aside, one can easily classify American architecture as initially Neo-Classic. Public buildings: state capitals, courthouses, city halls, post offices and public libraries, museums, churches or masonic temples are all Neo-Classical.
Washington is neo-classic!

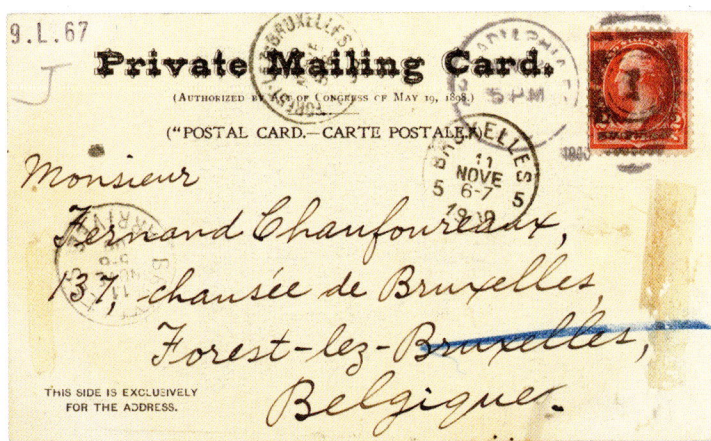

Fig. 5

Fig. 6

Fig. 7

5 & 6 The recto and verso of a 1900 postcard.

7 NORTH RIVER FERRIES, New York City, New York
Before the Holland Tunnel was built, there were 38 Manhattan ferry lines and access to New Jersey was available at 11 ferry points below 24th Street. The first Hoboken ferry was established in 1774; steam ferries appeared in 1814.

What is unusual is the scale of the buildings and the great freedom in the proportions of the components in relation to the original canons.

The designers of private buildings, while joyfully peppering pediments and columns about, interpreted a style which was well-tried and tested in France: an eclectic or Napoleonic (Napoleon III) style which is quite simply called the Beaux Arts style.

Architects such as Richard M. Hunt, Charles Follen McKim, Henry H. Richardson and Whitney Warren, all went to the School of Fine Arts in Paris, where the objective was to achieve beauty and not originality.

This freedom of expression gave free rein to historicism: famous revivals some in the Victorian style (Edward VII died in 1910), other Greek, Georgian (also known as Colonial or Mission style), Baroque and Rococo styles. You could write a whole chapter on Neo-Gothic revival alone and its multiple interpretations. But it is not too difficult to find your way about as the characteristics are clearly emphasised. The definition of the style is generally preceded by the word 'renaissance'.

Typical of the East Coast are the brownstones (first half of the 19th century). This kind of stone turns black in the rain. Brownstone decades encouraged a grotesque style in sculpture and also in architecture. Characteristic of the West Coast are its church outlines, which originated in South America.

It is a great pity that the fabulous cast-iron district of Soho, New York, with its fine examples of 'late Venetian elegance' was not included in any postcard collection - probably because its warehouses and factories were not 'noble enough'.

They are worth a visit. Their facades are very well preserved. You will not be disappointed.

The 1925 Decorative Arts Exhibition in Paris was a veritable mine of valuable information. The Art Deco period supplied a plethora of high quality edifices, buildings and skyscrapers, which seem just as fresh today as when they were built.

World War Two brought everything in Europe to a halt, including construction. Meanwhile in the United States Art Deco spread downwards to Miami where it metamorphosed into the Streamline Style, with its pastel-hued houses and hotels that are quite unique (image 9). All these styles (apart from cast-iron) are represented in postcard form. And all these sumptuous interpretations - true treasures - can still be seen today, as they were then, in American cities.

My collection stops in 1932 - the alleged date of the birth of the International style. It was at this very time that Henry-Russel Hitchcock and Philip Johnson (who brought Mies van der Rohe to the States) organised an architecture exhibition at the Museum Of Modern Art in New York.

WHAT ABOUT THE SKYSCRAPERS?

Skyscrapers in a nutshell: electricity, girders and elevators.

Previously, buildings could be no taller than five storeys and the rent fell as you went up.

The first office building incorporating hydraulic elevators in New York was the Equitable Building (designed by architects Gilman, Kendall and Post) in 1870. In Chicago, it was the Time and Life Building (by the architectural engineer, William LeBaron Jenney) in 1868.

The first non-gear wheel electric elevator made its appearance in 1903.

The skyscraper revolutionised the real-estate market. Initially, elevators travelled at a speed of 0.2 metres per second. Nowadays, they reach a speed of 12 metres per second.

The tight-knit patchwork of skyscrapers plunged the city into a series of dark canyons, and construction laws had to be drawn up to deal with the growing problem.

Once again, in 1915, the Equitable Building appeared in the limelight (image 10), when it was rebuilt on the ruins of the previous one (its architect was E.R.Graham) which had burnt down. It also sparked off the 1916 Zoning Resolution, adopted in 1922, which obliged building contractors to construct in a tiered fashion. A footnote explains that the total surface area was not allowed to exceed 12 times the surface area occupied at ground level. (The Equitable Building is 1,200,000 square feet in size - which equals 30 times its occupied ground surface!) Further amendments to the law were made, in particular covering the building site area. And, even later, it was added that buildings incorporating cultural activities were allowed to be taller.

The race for the tallest building goes on. The highly official list of the 100 tallest buildings in the world is updated on a daily basis.

Lastly, let us pause a while to remember the 'lost' buildings of America. In some places two, three or even four buildings were successively built on the same site. The postcard is sometimes the only living proof of their existence. Man-made (wilful and legalised destruction, arbitrary fires) and natural (earthquakes) disasters have destroyed many high quality buildings.

Six thousand postcards have to be stored in a chest, but *American Architecture: A Vintage Postcard Collection* can be a handy and constant companion on your bedside table.

Luc Van Malderen
Brussels, 1999

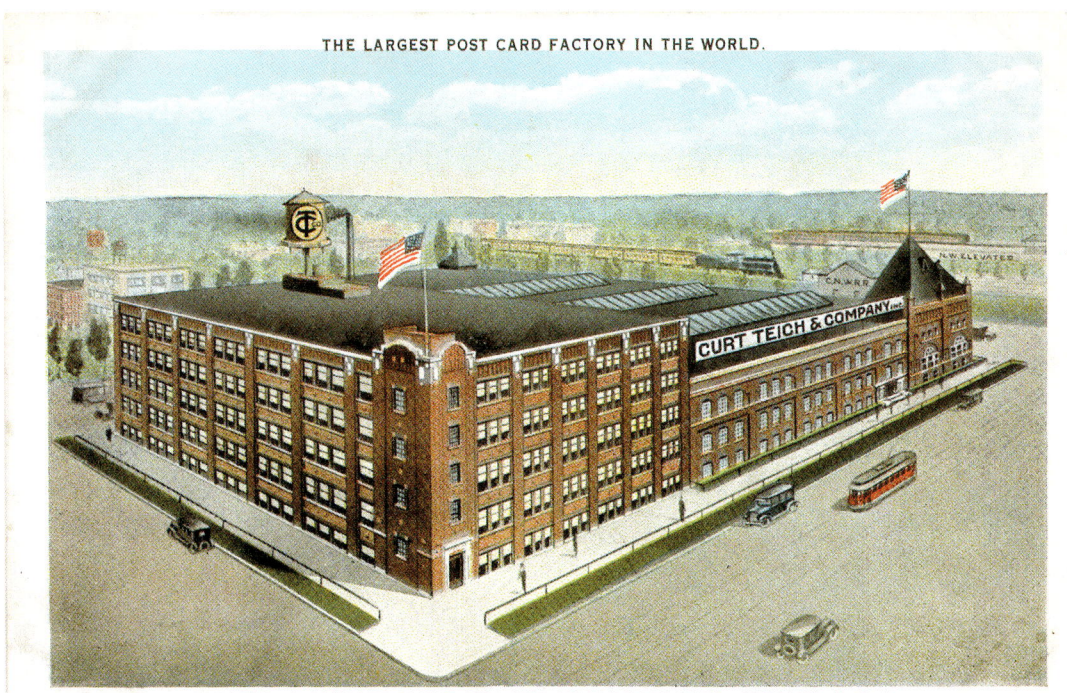

Fig. 8

Fig. 9

Fig. 10

8 Curt Teich probably invented the 'linen card'. This particular kind of embossing was done by calandering damp cardboard through a paper machine. The offset printing was curiously all the easier on such a surface. He boasted his factory was the largest postcard plant in the world, with 40 large printing presses and a thousand workers. I believe this to be true. The now silent factory houses archives and a museum.

9 OCEAN SURF HOTEL, Miami Beach, Florida
Fifty years ago, the summer rate for a single ocean-front room with a terrace was $6.00 and $7.00 for a double.
The other name for Streamline architecture is Tropical Deco, with its epicentre in Miami.

10 THE EQUITABLE BUILDING, New York City, New York
In 1916, four years after the three-day fire of the first Equitable Building, the new building reached completion: 540 feet, 38 storeys, with three below ground level, it houses 16,000 white-collar workers. The building was the last construction with no tiers before the 1916 Zoning Resolution.
It spans four city blocks and was the largest business structure in the world Major renovation took place in 1994-95.

1

Public School, Harmony, Pa.

2

1–6 The towns of the United States are peppered with a variety of curious, charming buildings with unexpected shapes. Countless city halls, courthouses, schools, railway stations, post offices and other public buildings bear witness to the never ending architectural saga, albeit in a sometimes very modest way.

Shown here are public buildings in Butler, Pennsylvania; Harmony, Pennsylvania; Alhambra, California; Beaumont, Texas; Bakersfield, California; and Charleston, South Carolina.

3

4

5

6

7

7–12 New Jersey: 80 miles of beach separated two seaside resorts, Ashbury Park and above all, Atlantic City, which in the twenties was extraordinary popular both with high society and the middle classes. Sadly in 1970, as their popularity died down, both the Hotel Traymore and the Malbourough-Blenheim were blown up. Then in 1976 seaside hotels became familiar again when their upkeep could be guaranteed by the legal introduction of gaming casinos.

8

9

10

84. HOTEL TRAYMORE AND BOARDWALK, ATLANTIC CITY, N. J.
11

12

13

14

ATLANTA, Georgia

13–14　In 1925 the Atlanta Convention Bureau boasted 101 hotels in town, and the back of another card stated that the city's elevators were hauling 179,308 passengers per day! Only a few of Atlanta's great buildings are depicted here.

15　GEORGIAN TERRACE HOTEL

16　FOURTH NATIONAL BANK BUILDING

17　HEALY SKYSCRAPER

18　THE WINECOFF HOTEL

GEORGIAN TERRACE HOTEL, ATLANTA, GA.

15

FOURTH NATIONAL BANK BUILDING, "FIVE POINTS," ATLANTA, GA.

16

HEALY SKY SCRAPER, ATLANTA, GA.

17

The Winecoff Hotel, Atlanta, Ga.

18

21

BALTIMORE AND OHIO BUILDING, BALTIMORE, MD.

19

BROMO SELTZER TOWER BUILDING.

NORTH-EAST CORNER EUTAW AND LOMBARD STREETS, BALTIMORE, MD.

20

Lord Baltimore Hotel
Hanover and Baltimore Streets
Baltimore, Md.

21

THE EMERSON
BALTIMORE AND CALVERT STREETS, BALTIMORE, MD.

22

23 NORTH WEST COR. BALTIMORE AND NORTH STREETS, BALTIMORE, MD. — MARYLAND CASUALTY TOWER BUILDING.

BALTIMORE, Maryland

- 19 BALTIMORE & OHIO BUILDING
- 20 BROMO SELTZER TOWER BUILDING
- 21 LORD BALTIMORE HOTEL
- 22 THE EMERSON HOTEL
- 23 MARYLAND CASUALTY TOWER BUILDING
- 24 HOTEL RENNERT
- 25 LEXINGTON STREET BUILDING

24 HOTEL RENNERT, BALTIMORE, MD.

25 LEXINGTON STREET BLDG., LEXINGTON AND LIBERTY STREETS. BALTIMORE, MD. Public Service Building Company, Owners. Built by J. Henry Miller, Inc.

BOSTON, Massachusetts

26–27 CUSTOM HOUSE
1837–47, architect A.B. Young, its site was the head of a long wharf. A four-faced Greek temple with a skylit dome. The 30-storey high tower above was built over the old building in 1913–15, architect Peabody & Stearns. Total height: 505 feet. It was once the highest building in New England.

28 FANUEIL HALL
1740–42, rebuilt 1762, rebuilt and enlarged 1805–06, architect C. Bulfinch. Restored 1898–99 and altered in 1979. It was the focus of the Revolutionary movement and therefore called the 'cradle of Liberty'.

The Market is now called Quincy Market. At the start an extension to the Fanueil Hall markets. A granite market house, two storeys high and 535 feet long, architect A. Parris. Today it houses the Tourist Information Office, a museum, post office and boutiques.

29 ELKS HOTEL
Now the Tremont Hotel opposite the Metropolitan Theater, it hosts a Wurlitzer pipe organ.

30 OLD STATE HOUSE
1712–13, rebuilt 1748, alteration I. Rogers; 1795–98, architect C. Bulfinch; 1830 restoration; 1881–82, architect G. Clough. On 18 July 1776 the Declaration of Independence was first read from its ceremonial balcony. Today it is the Boston History Museum.

31 HOTEL BREWSTER
Located in Boston's theatrical centre.

26

27

2886—Faneuil Hall, Boston, Mass.

28

ELKS HOTEL, 275 TREMONT STREET, BOSTON, MASS.

29

E 6422 OLD STATE HOUSE, BOSTON, MASS.

30

Hotel Brewster, Boston, Mass.

31

32

BOSTON, Massachusetts

32 THE NEW NORTH STATION
    The upper floors accommodate the Boston Garden, an immense arena seating about 18,500.
    On the right is the North Station Industrial Building, 14 storeys high, and on the left, the Hotel Manger.

33 THE SOUTH STATION,
    1899, architect Shepley, Rutan and Coolidge. A building of classical inspiration that continues to serve as the rail terminus linking Boston, Providence and New York. It has been restored several times.

34 PARK SQUARE BUILDING
    Now Park Plaza Hotel and offices.

35 SOUTH STATION and HOTEL ESSEX

36 THE OLD NORTH STATION

37 HOTEL COPLEY PLAZA
    1910–12, architect H. Hardenberg & C. Blackall. On the site of the old Art Museum. Today it belongs to the Sheraton chain.

33

34

35

36

37

38

39

40

41

42

38   REDMONT HOTEL, Birmingham, Alabama
39   CLARIDGE HOTEL, Atlantic City, New York
40   MONTICELLO HOTEL, Charlottesville, Virginia
41   HOTEL BARNUM, Bridgeport, Connecticut

BUFFALO, New York

42   ELECTRIC BUILDING
43   CITY HALL, architect J. Wade, 1929

43

44

45

BUFFALO, New York

44 MASTEN PARK HIGH SCHOOL

45 MANUFACTURERS AND TRADERS BANK

46 STATE OFFICE BUILDING and FEDERAL BUILDING with the LIBERTY BANK BUILDING in the background

46

47

47 GRAIN ELEVATORS
48 HOTEL GRAYSTONE
49 ELLICOT SQUARE BUILDING

48

49

50

51

50–55 Whether for road or rail, the entire country is full of bridges with striking structures.
A relevant inventory of these would need another volume.

52

THE GREAT DRAW-SPAN OPEN IN K. & I. BRIDGE, BETWEEN LOUISVILLE, KY. AND NEW ALBANY, IND.

53

936—The Grand Canyon Navajo Bridge across the Colorado River at Lee's Ferry

54

"ON THE CHICAGO, MILWAUKEE & ST. PAUL RAILWAY."

MISSOURI RIVER BRIDGE AT MOBRIDGE, S. DAK.

55

CHICAGO, Illinois

56–58
MERCHANDISE MART
1923–31, architects Graham, Anderson, Probst & White. More than four million square feet of floor space. The world's largest building until the completion of the Pentagon near Washington, DC. Built as a wholesale store by Marshall Field & Co, today it is a gigantic display centre. It was renovated in 1992.

59 PURE OIL BUILDING
1924–26, architects Thielbar & Fugard with Giaver & Dinkelberg. This beautiful forbear was based on the fifteenth century chapel of the Certosa of Pavia. It is clad with decorative terracotta tiles. A 17-storey tower rises from a 24-storey base and is capped with a belvedere. In the central core the developers included a garage, accessible by elevator. Converted to office space in 1940. In the beginning the building was the Jewellers Building, today it is known by its address: 35 East Wacker's Drive.

Chicago — Columbus Memorial Building

60

Chicago — Old Colony Building

Louisa C. Blatt

61

Chicago

62

Chicago

63

64

GREAT OLD TIMERS:

60 COLUMBUS MEMORIAL BUILDING

61 OLD COLONY BUILDING, 1893–94, architect Holabird & Roche, 17 storeys

62 TRIBUNE BUILDING

63 MONADNOCK BUILDING, 1891–93, architects Burnham & Root and Holabird & Roche

64 CHAMPLAIN BUILDING AND BOSTON STORE (Powers Building), 1903, architect Holabird & Roche

65 GREAT NORTHERN BUILDING

66 CHICAGO SAVINGS BANK BUILDING (Chicago Building), 1903, architect Holabird & Roche

65

66

67

68

67–69 THE LOOP, Chicago, Illinois
The loop's elevated train is a powerful symbol of Chicago. The very first loop was created with cable car turnabouts in 1882. The present loop was built between 1892 and 1908. The first electrically-powered lines were opened in 1897. The loop has avoided being dismantled as the urbanity it generates is essential to the city.

69

70 MARSHALL FIELD & CO'S RETAIL STORE, Chicago, Illinois.

71

71 MARSHALL FIELD & CO'S RETAIL STORE, Chicago, Illinois
1892, architect D. Burnham.
1906, architect D. Burnham & Co.
1914, architect Graham, Burnham & Co.
In 1885–87 architect H. Richardson built the first Marshall Field wholesale store and warehouse building. It was demolished in 1930.

72 ROTHSCHILD STORE, Chicago, Illinois
1906 and addition in 1910, architect Holabird & Roche. Another four floors were added in 1928 by architect A. Alschuler.

73 SIEGEL, COOPER & CO, Chicago, Illinois
This building later became the Sears, Roebuck & Co. store and is today the second Leiter Building. 1891, arch. W. LeBaron Jenney, eight storeys, 553,000 square feet.
A modern building with steel, cast iron and glass, it was subdivided in 1981.

74 & 76
THE FAIR STORE, Chicago, Illinois
1890–91, architect W. LeBaron Jenney. Business began in 1875 in a store 16 x 80 feet. Fifteen years later the facade measured 1,080 feet with a floor space of 677,500 square feet. The building has been demolished.

75 THE BOSTON STORE, Chicago, Illinois
1912–17, architect Holabird & Roche. Today called the State-Madison Building.

72

73

74

75

76

77

78

77–82 The Chicago River with its succession of bridges and the fabulous buildings erected over a century on its banks makes the river a unique sight, probably the richest twentieth architectural plot on earth.

79

80

43

81

82

83–85 NORTH MICHIGAN AVENUE BRIDGE
1918–20, architect H. Bennett and engineer T. Pihlfeldt & H. Young. This double deck bridge was inaugurated in 1920; it immediately changed the urbanity of the whole neighbourhood. The bascule bridge is capable of handling two levels of traffic and still clearing the channel in under 60 seconds.

86 BRIDGE HOUSES
1924–28, architect H. Bennett with sculptures by J. Fraser and H. Herring.

83

84

85

86

87

88

89

90

91

93

92

94

(From previous pages)

87–88
THE CHICAGO TRIBUNE TOWER, Chicago, Illinois
1923–25, architect Hood and Howells, 36 storeys, 460 feet.
In 1922 the Chicago Tribune announced what became one of the twentieth century's famous architectural competitions: $100,000 in prize money to design its new headquarters adjacent to the Tribune's new printing plant on the Chicago River (architect J. Hunt, 1916–20). The 264 competition entries that flooded in from around the world were to influence American architecture. The prize winner designed a Gothic tower with an octagonal top. It is now a designated landmark.
Just behind is the MEDINAH ATHLETIC CLUB (now the Hotel Intercontinental Chicago), 1929, architect W. Ahlschlager. A Neo-Egyptian revival and romantic historicism building.

89–90
THE WRIGLEY BUILDING, Chicago, Illinois
1919–22, architect Graham, Anderson, Probst & White, 398 feet. North annex building (1925) connected by an upper-level skywalk. White terracotta cladding gives the building a brilliant look day and night. The buildings were constructed on a small and irregular plot next to the Michigan Avenue Bridge on the Chicago River. A designated landmark.

91–92
PALMOLIVE BUILDING, Chicago, Illinois
1929, architect Holabird & Root, 37 storeys, 468 feet. A shining example of the Art Deco style, with setbacks in conformity due to the 1923 zoning law. For 50 years it had a powerful beacon to guide aerial and maritime traffic, eventually it became a nuisance as other towers arose nearby. Today known by its address, 919 North Michigan Avenue, it was formerly the Playboy Building.

92–93
BOARD OF TRADE, Chicago, Illinois
1930, architect Holabird & Root, 45-storey limestone Art Deco skyscraper, 605 feet.
Originally initiated in one room on March 13, 1848, the Board of Trade occupied a wigwam immediately after the Great Fire in 1871. A building designed by W. Boyington was erected on the same spot in 1871. Then came the 1885–89 Board of Trade designed by Bauman & Huehl and Richardson. The new adjoining building was built in 1980, architect H. Jahn, a 24 storey addition.

95–96
BOARD OF TRADE, Chicago, Illinois
The 1885–89 building designed by architects Bauman & Huehl and Richardson and the present one looking down La Salle Street.

97 ONE LA SALLE STREET BUILDING, Chicago, Illinois
It seems street numbers have changed in La Salle Street. This building corresponds to the 1934 La Salle Bank Building (architect Graham, Anderson, Probst & White) with 49 storeys and four below the ground.

98 WILLOUGBY TOWER and MONTGOMERY WARD & Co BUILDING, Chicago, Illinois
1929, architect S. Crowen & Associates.
1897–99, architect R. Schmidt.

99 PEOPLE'S GAS COMPANY BUILDING, Chicago, Illinois
1910, architect Burnham & Co, 22 storeys. The central light court opens above the third floor. The whole of the building is clad with terracotta.

100 FIELD BUILDING, Chicago, Illinois
1928–34, architect Graham, Anderson, Probst & White. Located on the site of William LeBaron Jenney's home. Insurance Building designed by P. Shaw, four 22-storey wings surround a central 43-storey shaft. It was the last building built in the loop over the following 20 years (due to the Wall Street Crash).

95

96

348 ONE LA SALLE STREET BUILDING, CHICAGO

97

365 WILLOUGBY TOWER, MICHIGAN AVENUE AND MADISON STREET, CHICAGO

98

569C. Peoples Gas Light and Coke Building, Chicago.

99

150—Field Building, Chicago

100

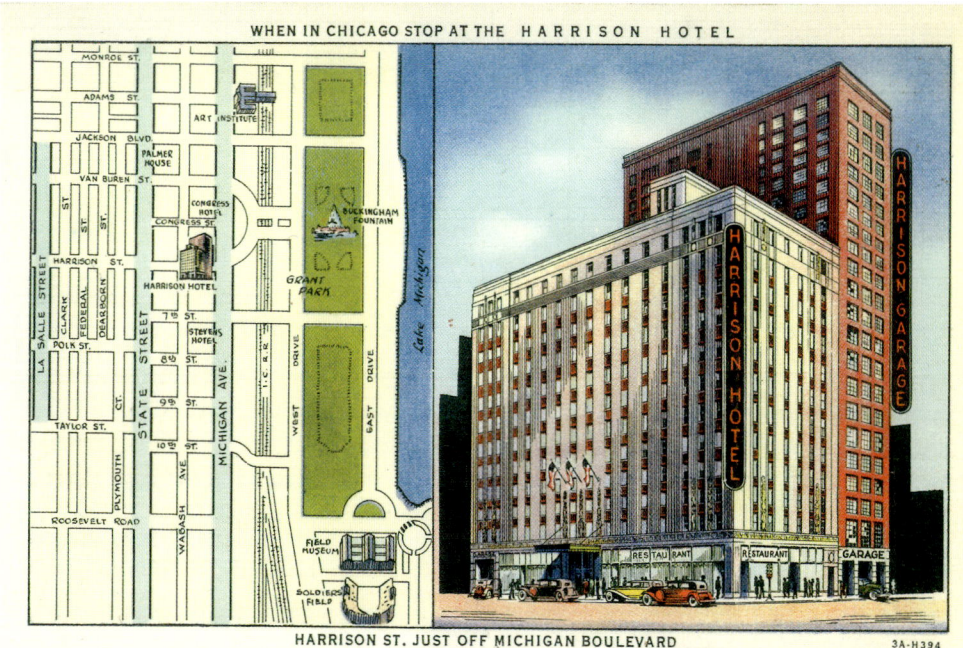

101

102

101 HARRISON HOTEL, Chicago, Illinois

102-103
  THE DRAKE HOTEL, Chicago, Illinois
  1919, architect Marshall & Fox, 800 rooms, 15 storeys. Inspired by Italian renaissance palazzi. Particularities: large family apartments and a bachelors' floor.

103

104

105

104–105
STEVENS HOTEL, Chicago, Illinois
1922–27, architect Holabird & Roche, 25 storeys, 3,000 outside rooms. Built to be the world's 'largest and most sumptuous' hotel with a convention hall seating 4,000, an exhibition hall, and a rooftop golf course. In 1942 the War Department used the hotel as a barracks. In 1945 it was acquired by Conrad Hilton, and is today called the Chicago Hilton & Towers. Renovated 1986.

106

107

106 HOTEL BELMONT, 650 outside rooms.

108

107–110

HOTEL MORRISON, Chicago, Illinois

There have been successive enlargements of the Morrison. This huge hotel – 46 storeys – housed a terrace garden, 1,944 outside rooms and 3,400 rooms when completed (400 located in the towers).

109

110

111 ALLERTON HOTEL, Chicago, Illinois
1924, architects Murgatroyd & Ogden, Fugard & Knapp, 25 storeys, 253 feet. It was first called Allerton House and catered to young, professional men and women.

112 HOTEL SHERMAN, Chicago, Illinois

113 BLACKSTONE HOTEL, Chicago, Illinois
1908, architect Marshall & Fox, 20 storeys. A French Second Empire style hotel and the first high-rise hotel built on Michigan Avenue. The cabaret Mayfair room closed in 1956.
The Blackstone was famous for the personalities who stayed there.

114 PALMER HOUSE, Chicago, Illinois
1925, architect Holabird & Roche, 2,268 guest rooms, 23 storeys. A creation of Potter Palmer. This is the fourth Palmer House, the first and second were destroyed by the 1871 Great Fire, the third was disrated. The Empire Room was particularly used for Sunday brunches.

115 HOTEL LA SALLE
1909, architect Holabird & Roche. The building has been demolished.

116–117 Y.M.C.A. HOTEL, Chicago, Illinois
1916, architect R. Berlin with J. Rogers, 2,400 rooms. It was converted to apartments in 1988.

114

115

116

117

118

119

118–119
AUDITORIUM BUILDING AND HOTEL, Chicago, Illinois
1889, architect Adler & Sullivan. The Auditorium seated 4,237. Dismantled in 1953. Today it belongs to the Roosevelt University and is a cultural and architectural landmark.

120 CONGRESS HOTEL, Chicago, Illinois
1893, architect C. Warren, 1902–07 Holabird & Roche.

120

121

122

121 SHERIDAN-PLAZA HOTEL

122 GREAT NORTHERN HOTEL, Chicago, Illinois
     1892, architect Burnham & Root, 22 storeys, 290 feet. Demolished in 1940.

123 CHATELAINE TOWER
     An apartment building with three, four and five room apartments and eight room duplexes.

123

124 FIVE STRUCTURES ON SOUTH MICHIGAN AVENUE, Chicago, Illinois
PEOPLE'S GAS BUILDING, 1911, architect D. Burnham & Co.
LAKE VIEW BUILDING (Municipal Court Building), 1906–12, architect Jenney, Mundie & Jensen
ILLINOIS ATHLETIC CLUB (former), 1908, Barnett Haynes & Barnett
MONROE BUILDING, 1912, architect Holabird & Roche
UNIVERSITY CLUB, 1908–09, architect Holabird & Roche

125 CITY HALL AND COUNTY BUILDING, Chicago, Illinois
1907–11, architect Holabird & Roche, 11 storeys. After the Chicago fire of 1871 a massive City Hall/County Building was designed by J. Egan and completed in 1885 but was demolished 20 years later. The new building has been in use for more than 90 years now, a testament to its functionality and symbolic civic virtues.

126 AMERICAN FURNITURE MART, Chicago, Illinois
1924–26, architects G. Nimmons & Co and M. Dunning. East: 16 storeys, west: 23 storeys. The tower is Gothic and is inspired by the Houses of Parliament, London. Today called Lake Shore Palace, it is a mixed-use building comprising apartments, offices, parking and stores.

127 CHICAGO TEMPLE, Chicago, Illinois
1922–23, architect Holabird & Roche, 21-storey commercial office tower. Above the office block is an eight-storey Gothic spire that houses the 'chapel in the sky'. Altogether 556 feet, but the Temple is on the two first floors.

128 NEW MASONIC TEMPLE, Chicago, Illinois
The building has 22 storeys, two basements and a theatre seating 3,000.

129 MASONIC TEMPLE, Chicago, Illinois
1892, architect Burnham & Roots, 22 storeys, 354 feet, destroyed in 1939.

124

125

126

127

128

129

130

130–132
UNION STATION, Chicago, Illinois
1913–25, architect Graham, Anderson, Probst & White. Of the eight railway stations in Chicago, Union Station is the last to survive. The huge travertine-clad waiting room in the farther away structure and the 8-storey office tower, which was meant to be 20 storeys as in the lower postcard, are still there but the concourse of the nearby station depot was demolished in 1969. The upper postcard is a fake. The plan allows trains to move in either direction at either end to a total of 720 trains a day.

133 DEARBORN STATION, Chicago, Illinois
1885, architect C. Eidlitz, reconstructed after the fire. Chicago's oldest train station, it was converted in 1983.

134 CHICAGO & NORTHWESTERN RAILROAD STATION, Chicago, Illinois
1911, architect Frost & Granger. Demolished.

135 LA SALLE STREET STATION
Demolished but the La Salle Street commuters' station is still there.

131

132

133

134

135

136–137
WHITE CITY ENTRANCE, Chicago, Illinois
The 1893 World's Columbian Exposition (called the White City) had a powerful and lasting impact on Chicago's urban development. W. Root was selected as the architect in charge of design and his partner D. Burnham was to be chief of construction. The architecture was very much influenced by the Ecole des Beaux Arts in Paris. The Palace of Fine Arts was saved to become the Museum of Science and Industries in 1933 (D. Burnham & Co) with major reconstruction in 1929–40. The style of the exposition was baptised 'Imperial Roman'.

138–140
FEDERAL BUILDING and POST OFFICE, Chicago, Illinois
1897–1905, architect H. Cobb. Occupied a full city square, 311 x 386 feet. The main building is eight storeys high and the dome rises to 297 feet. Knocked down in 1966.

141 The dome of the Post Office and Government Building on completion.

136

137

138

An interesting moment during construction of the Post Office and Government Bldg.

141

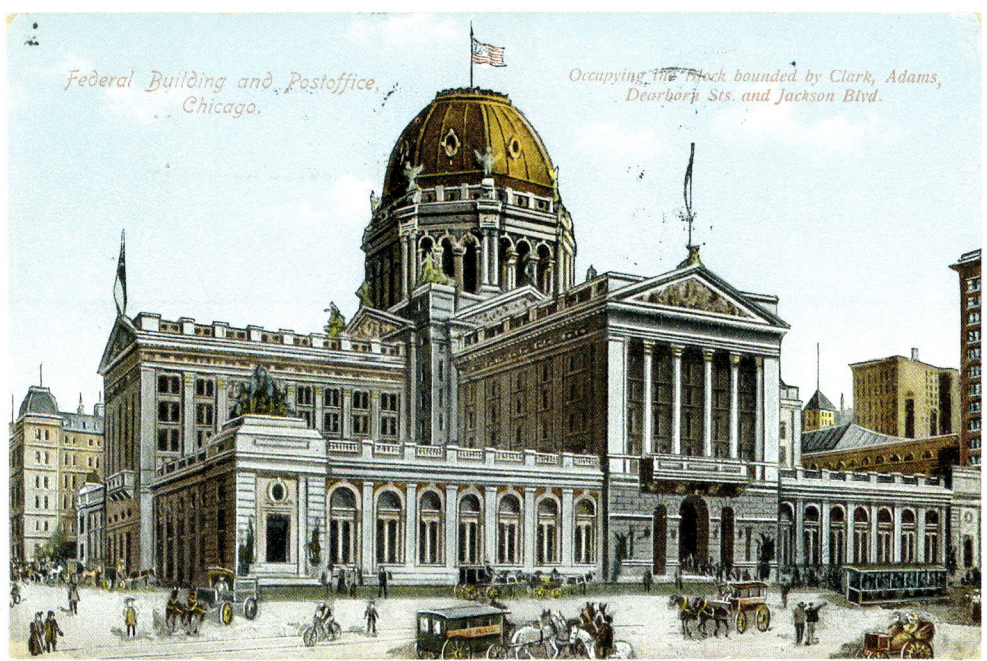

139

140

142

143

144

145

376. CONTINENTAL & COMMERCIAL BANK BUILDING, CHICAGO.

142   CHICAGO DAILY NEWS BUILDING, Chicago, Illinois

1925–29, architect Holabird & Root, 25 storeys. Headquarters of the old Chicago Daily News. The first building in Chicago to use air rights above railroad tracks. This was achieved by using large double 12-foot girders to cantilever parts of the building. Today it is Riverside Plaza.

143   THE FIRST NATIONAL BANK BUILDING, Chicago, Illinois

Architect Burnham & Co. This was the site of the bank before it moved to Madison Avenue in 1969.

144   CIVIC OPERA BUILDING, Chicago, Illinois

1927–29, architect Graham, Anderson, Probst & White, 567 feet, 42 storeys. A complex structure housing the auditorium of the Opera House, the Civic Theatre and a 45-storey office building. The previous opera house was constructed by Cobb & Frost and demolished in 1912.

145   LONDON GUARANTEE & ACCIDENT BUILDING, Chicago, Illinois

1922–23, architect S. Alshuler, 22 storey Indiana limestone building. A Beaux Arts construction with a Greco-Roman tempietto on the historic site of Fort Dearborn. Today it is the Stone Container Building.

146   CONTINENTAL & COMMERCIAL BANK BUILDING, Chicago, Illinois

1914, architect Graham, Burnham & Co, 21 storeys, 323 x 166 x 260 feet high.

In the basement were 20,000 safes. Today it is known as the 208 S. La Salle Street Building.

147 LAKE STREET BRIDGE

148 GRAIN ELEVATOR

149 HIBBARD, SPENCER, BARTLETT & Co (wholesale hardware)

150–152 GRAIN ELEVATORS in Minneapolis, Chicago and Buffalo (DAKOTA ELEVATORS, 1900–14).

Lake Street Bridge, Chicago

147

Chicago
One of Armours Grain Elevators

148

Chicago, Ill. Hibbard, Spencer, Bartlett & Co. (Wholesale Hardware).

149

150

151

152

153

154

CINCINNATI, Ohio

153–154
: CINCINNATI UNION TERMINAL
  1930–33, architects Fellheimer & Wagner with P. Cret. The most majestic of the five Art Deco terminal stations. Today it is a museum centre.

155 SUSPENSION BRIDGE over OHIO RIVER

156 THE UNION CENTRAL LIFE INSURANCE Co. BUILDING

157 HOTEL SINTON

158 NETHERLAND PLAZA HOTEL
  1930, architects W. Ahlschlager with Delano & Aldrich, 31 storeys. It was erected in 13 months and restored in 1982–92.

159 INGALLS BUILDING

155

THE UNION CENTRAL LIFE INSURANCE CO. BUILDING, CINCINNATI, OHIO.

156

HOTEL SINTON—ST. NICHOLAS, CINCINNATI, OHIO

FIREPROOF—ACCOMMODATING 1,500 GUESTS

157

Netherland Plaza Hotel, 5th and Race Streets, Cincinnati, Ohio

158

INGALLS BUILDING, CINCINNATI, OHIO.

159

160

161

162

163

THE NEW UNION STATION. CLEVELAND, OHIO. HOTEL CLEVELAND.

164

The Hotel Euclid, Cleveland, Ohio.

165

73 Cleveland Public Auditorium, showing Terminal Tower, Cleveland, Ohio

166

CLEVELAND, Ohio

- 160 WILLIAMSON BUILDING
- 161 THE CLEVELAND DISCOUNT BUILDING
- 162 THE CLEVELAND ATHLETIC CLUB
- 163 THE ROCKEFELLER BUILDING
- 164 THE UNION STATION and HOTEL
- 165 HOTEL EUCLID
- 166 CLEVELAND AUDITORIUM
  Fourteen events can be held simultaneously seating 13,156 in the Auditorium, 3,000 in the Music Hall, 1,500 each in the Ball Room and the Exhibition Hall, 200 in the Little Theatre, as well as more people in several additional halls.

167

168

169

170

171

172

DALLAS, Texas

167 MEDICAL ARTS BUILDING
Built in 1923, it was once the tallest reinforced concrete structure in Texas. Demolished in 1977.

168 GREAT SOUTHERN LIFE BUILDING
1914, purported architects for Story 1 and 2: Lang & Winchell. The third to eleventh storeys were added in 1917.

169 BAKER HOTEL
A 1925 unit of the Baker Hotel System of Texas (San Antonio, Austin, Forth Worth). Demolished in 1979.

170 DALLAS, Main Street Canyon

171–172
HOTEL ADOLPHUS
Two views of the hotel.
1912, architect T. Barnett & Haynes. The St. Louis 'Beer Baron' Adolphus Bush opened the hotel in 1912. It had 825 rooms and 19 storeys in the Beaux Arts style. The 22-storey tower is capped by a bronze dome and a lantern. Sold in 1980 to California Investment.

DETROIT, Michigan

173–175
During navigation season eight millions passengers arrive and depart from Detroit.

176 DIME SAVINGS BANK BUILDING
1910, architect D.H. Burnham, 23 storeys. This particularly refined and well decorated skyscraper was erected on the site of the Walker building.

177 DAVID WHITNEY BUILDING
1915, architect Baxter, O'Dell & Halpin.

178 DETROIT NATIONAL BANK & CENTRAL SAVINGS BANK
Now called the New Bank, it was erected on the site of the historic Pontchartrain with 24 storeys and four below.

179 FORD BUILDING
1909, architect Baxter, O'Dell & Halpin, 18 storeys, 250 feet.

173

174

175

176 Dime Savings Bank Building, Detroit, Mich.

177 David Whitney Building, Detroit, Mich.

178 New Bank and Office Building of the First and Old Detroit National Bank, Central Savings Bank and First National Co., Detroit, Mich.

179 Ford Building, Detroit, Mich.

180

181

DETROIT, Michigan

180   HOTEL FORT SHELBY
The hotel has 22 storeys, 900 rooms and a remarkable view of Detroit with the river and Canada beyond.

181   BOOK CADILLAC HOTEL
There are 1,200 guest rooms, and four restaurants including the Book Casino.

182   HOTEL PONTCHARTRAIN
1907–16, architect G. Mason, 15 storeys and three underground. The 24-storey First National Bank (architect A. Kahn) was constructed in 1922 on the site.

183–184
PENOBSCOT BUILDING
1927–28, architect W. Rowland. The entry arch is five storeys high. This was Detroit's tallest skyscraper. On the top of the building is a Mayan light aeroplane beacon!

185   HOTEL STATLER
1914–15, architect G.B. Post. The entire second floor is given to banquet rooms, ballrooms and a convention hall. Two floors are sample rooms. Later it became the Detroit Hilton with 800 rooms and five classes of rooms at varying prices.

186   VINTON BUILDING and FIRST NATIONAL BANK BUILDING
The National Bank was erected on the site of Hotel Pontchartrain on Cadillac Square, 1922, architect A. Kahn.

182

204— PENOBSCOT BUILDING, DETROIT, MICH.

183

563:—Penobscot Building At Night, Detroit, Mich.

184

HOTEL STATLER
DETROIT
1000 ROOMS   1000 BATHS

185

VINTON BLDG. AND FIRST NATIONAL BANK. BLDG.

DETROIT, MICH.

186

77

DETROIT, Michigan

187–188
: GENERAL MOTORS OFFICE BUILDING
  1920–22, architects A. Kahn & Henry Ford. It covers an area of 504 x 322 feet and is 15 storeys high with 24 elevators, 1,650 offices and, of course, houses its beautiful display of automobiles such as Chevrolets, Buicks, Pontiacs, Oldsmobiles and Cadillacs.

189 THE MICHIGAN CENTRAL STATION,
  1913, architect Warren & Wetmore. Covers 21 acres with eleven tracks in the station.
  The old first station was erected in 1893 by architect J. Stewart & Co.

190–191
: THE FISHER BUILDING
  1928, architect A. Kahn. Inspired by the striking array of the Fisher Theater with its imitations of Mayan architecture. The tower is lit at night.

192 THE BOOK TOWER
  1926, architect L. Kamper, 475 feet, 36 storeys, 900 offices and 70 shops.

193 EATON TOWER (on the left), architect L. Kamper, and DAVID WHITNEY BUILDING (on the right)

187

188

189

190

191

192

193

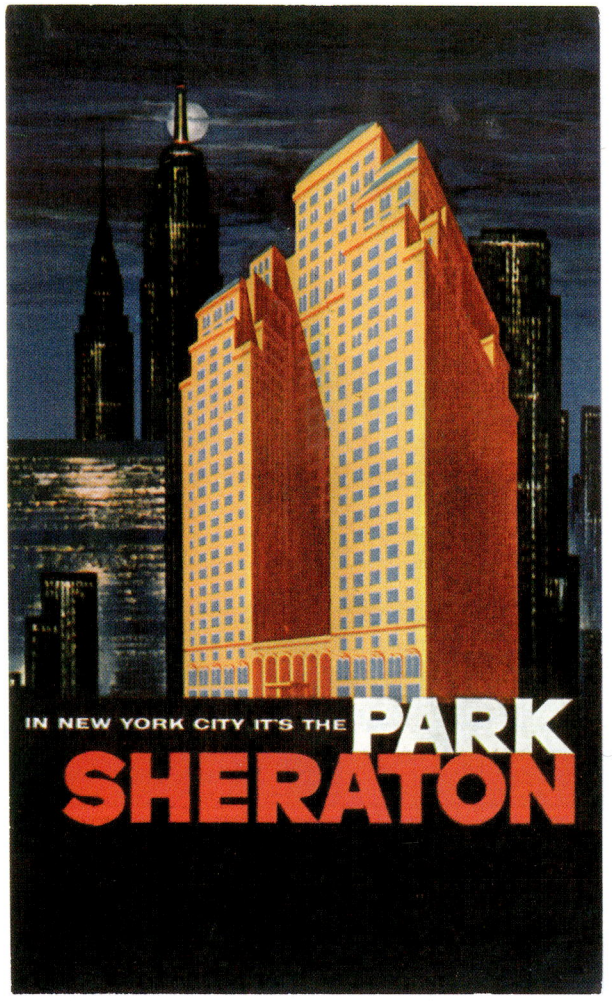
194

195

196

197

98

194–199
It is quite amusing to see some well-known hotel structures that are now run under the Sheraton banner. These cards were edited in the 1940s.

99

DENVER, Colorada

200 MUNICIPAL AUDITORIUM
Seating capacity: 12,000 (can be subdivided).

201 HOTEL COSMOPOLITAN, 1926

202 NORTH DENVER HIGH SCHOOL

EL PASO, Texas

203 BASSETT TOWER

204 MASONIC TEMPLE

205 TWO REPUBLICS LIFE BUILDING

206 HOTEL PASO DEL NORTE

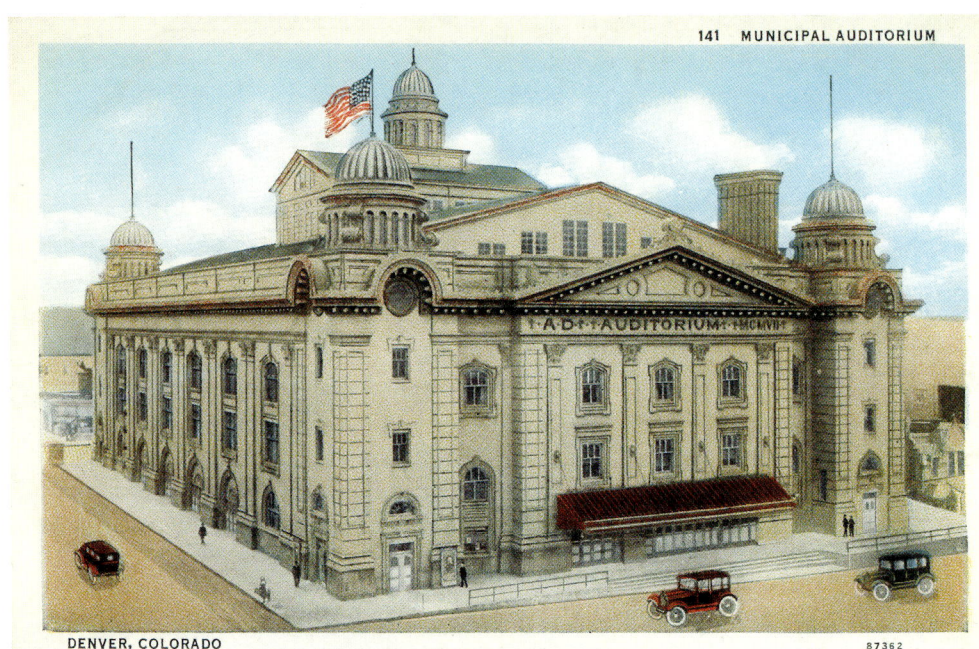

200

201

202

203

204

205

206

207

208

209

210

211

212

207 FIRST NATIONAL BANK, Charleroi, Pennsylvania
208 ELKS CLUB, Galveston, Texas
209 EAGLE'S HOME, Galveston, Texas
210 THE HEXAGON, Mineral Wells, Texas
211 CHITTENDEN HOTEL, Columbus, Ohio
212 PLAZA HOTEL, Port Arthur, Texas
213 WILTSHIRE HOTEL, Atlantic City, New Jersey

213

85

GRAND RAPIDS, Michigan

  214   MORTON HOTEL

  215   GRAND RAPIDS NATIONAL BANK

  216   GRAND RAPIDS TRUST COMPANY BANK

  217–219
      Three Grand Rapids downtown views.

214

215

216

PEARL STREET BRIDGE, GRAND RAPIDS, MICH.

217

LOOKING WEST ON MONROE AVENUE, GRAND RAPIDS, MICHIGAN

218

Monroe Avenue Looking West, Grand Rapids, Mich.

219

220–226
In the 1930s a number of buildings had colour illumination, and sometimes Lindbergh beacons. These beams of light were supposed to guide aeroplanes or ships entering the harbour, but the main idea was to attract attention to the buildings.

220

221

222

223

224

225

226

227

228

229

230

231

232

233

HOUSTON, Texas

227 The heart of Houston, from left to right: NIELS ESPERSON BUILDING, the ESPERSON SECOND NATIONAL BANK and GULF BUILDING.

228 GULF BUILDING by night

229 TEXAS STATE HOTEL, 400 rooms

230 POST-DISPATCH BUILDING

231 THE ESPERSON BUILDINGS

232 THE HOUSTON YMCA is ten stories high and built in what could be called Italian Renaissance style.

233 THE RICE HOTEL (1,000 rooms) was built on the site of the first capitol building of the Republic of Texas, 1838.

234

234 HOTEL MASON, Jacksonville, Florida

235 HOTEL SEMINOLE, Jacksonville, Florida

236 OLDS TOWER BUILDING,
Lansing, Michigan

237 FAYETTE NATIONAL BANK,
Lexington, Kentucky

238 DESHLER WALLICK HOTEL (1916),
THEATER and A.I.U. Citadel (45 storeys),
Columbus, Ohio

239 FIRST NATIONAL BANK,
Davenport, Louisiana

235

236

237

238

239

LOS ANGELES, California

240–241
    CITY HALL
    1928, architect Austin, Parkinson, Martin & Whittlesey.

242 LA.56 WARNER BROTHERS WESTERN THEATER

243 RICHFIELD OIL COMPANY BUILDING
    Clad entirely with black and gold tiles. An aviation beacon of 40 million candle power on top.

244 LA.50 BROADWAY

245 HOTEL HAYWARD
    Four other hotels in California under the same management.

240

241

242

243

244

245

246 THE AUDITORIUM, Los Angeles, California

247 LOS ANGELES BILTMORE, Los Angeles, California

1923, architect Schultze & Weaver (who built the new Waldorf Astoria in New York).

Miss Vada Heilman checked 4,400 keys at the opening of the 13 storeys. Remodelled in 1987.

248 NEW ROSSLYN HOTELS, Los Angeles, California

Twin hotels connected by marble subway, 1,100 rooms.

249–252

An oil tank and a derrick on fire next to an oil and a water gusher, the 'Old Faithful' geyser in Yellowstone Park, Wyoming.

246

247

248

249

250

251

252

253

253–254 GREYHOUND BUS TERMINALS in the 30s, architect W. Arrasmith
Cleveland, Ohio and Baltimore, Maryland

255 HOE SAI GAI RESTAURANT, Dearborn, Illinois

254

255

256

257

258

256 UNITED STATES POST OFFICE and COURT HOUSE, Norfolk, Virginia (1933)

257 UNITED STATES POST OFFICE, Atlanta, Georgia

258 CHICAGO POST OFFICE, Illinois (1933)
The structure spans the railroad tracks leading into the Union Railway Station. The flat roof, 790 x 200 feet, is designed for use as an aeroplane landing field. There were 7,000 workers employed in the building to handle 6,500,000 letters and circulars each week.

259

THE ART DECO DISTRICT, Miami Beach, Florida

The story goes that a ship named the Providencia, carrying a cargo of coconuts from Havana to Barcelona, was wrecked here and that is how the local vegetation got started. Between 1910 and 1924 the town population grew from 5,000 to 100,000 inhabitants.

The rush on Miami dates from 1920: 84 Art Deco buildings were constructed between 1930 and 1940. But the town's official birth date is 1896 when Henri Flager, oil king, introduced the railroad at the invitation of Julia Tuttle, and built the Royal Palm Beach Hotel. The District has been registered as a site of historic interest since 1979.

- 259 DADE COUNTY COURT HOUSE and MIAMI CITY HALL, Miami, Florida

- 260 EVERGLADES HOTEL, Miami Beach, Florida
  Built in 1926, it was initially called the Roney Plaza Hotel then the Hotel Biltmore. The tower is a replica of the Giralda, Seville. Once Al Capone occupied the 13th floor.

- 261 LUMMUS PARK, Miami Beach, Florida

- 262 BREAKWATER HOTEL, Miami Beach, Florida

- 263 BEACON HOTEL, Miami Beach, Florida

260

261

262

263

MIAMI BEACH, Florida

264 COLLINS AVENUE HOTELS
265 DOWNTOWN MIAMI BEACH
266 LUMMUS PARK

264

265

266

267

268

268–269
MILWAUKEE, Wisconsin
Around 1910 the PABST BREWERY was the world's largest. The SCHLITZ BREWERY comes in second and the writer says it is only 'half as large'.

MINNEAPOLIS, Minnesota

270 THE FOSHAY TOWER,
1927–29, architect L. Arnal for Magney & Tusler, 447 feet. A 30-storey concrete Art Deco skyscraper with sloping sides.
271 TELEPHONE BUILDING
272 M.58 RAND TOWER

270

271

272

273

274

275

Some examples of the grand Neo-classic aspiration of public buildings.

273 STATE EDUCATIONAL BUILDING, Albany, New York

274 OHIO NATIONAL BANK BUILDING, Columbus, Ohio

275 NORTH WESTERN MUTUAL LIFE INSURANCE CO. BUILDING, Milwaukee, Wisconsin

276

276 THE GEORGIAN HOTEL, Evanston, Illinois

277 THE PANTLIND HOTEL, Grand Rapids, Michigan
The publicity announces a full floor of seven-foot beds for tall people!

278 HOTEL INDIANA, Indiana, Pennsylvania

277

278

279

280

279 HOTEL BRUNSWICK, Lancaster, Pennsylvania
From the balcony of Cadwell House occupying this site, Abraham Lincoln addressed the people of Lancaster, 22 February 1861, on his way to Washington for his first inauguration.

280 ST. CHARLES HOTEL, New Orleans, Louisiana

281

282

283

NEWARK, New Jersey

281 LEFCOURT BUILDING and NATIONAL NEWARK & ESSEX BANKING CO.

282 BAMBERGER & CO. DEPARTMENT STORE

283 THE NATIONAL NEWARK BUILDING

284 ESSEX COUNTY COURTHOUSE

285 THE BAMBERGER BUILDING

286 PUBLIC LIBRARY

284

285

286

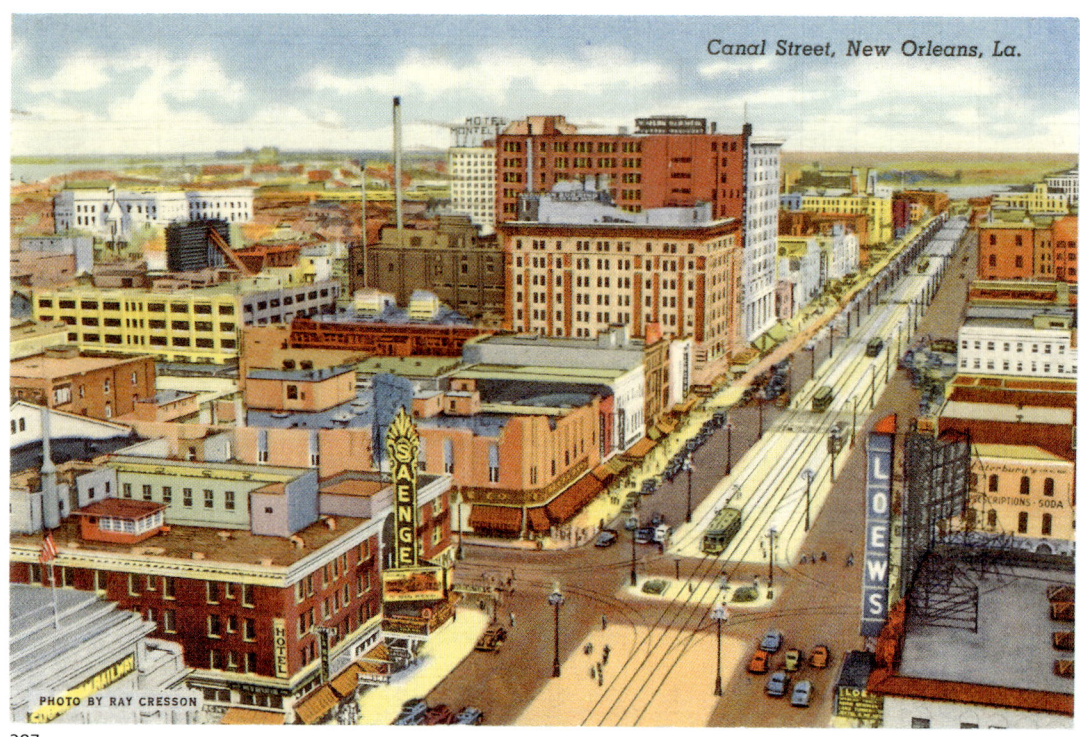
287

288

NEW ORLEANS, Louisiana

287–288
    CANAL STREET

289 HIBERNIA BANK BUILDING
    1921, 355 feet, 23 storeys, capped with a lantern. The light in the tower of the building is chartered as an official lighthouse by the United States government.

290 HOTEL DE SOTO

291 COTTON EXCHANGE

292 HOTEL GRUNEWALD
    1893, rebuilt in 1908. In 1925 it was named the Roosevelt Hotel and in 1937 it became the 'Blue Room' nightclub. From 1938 to 1940 it was an 'oasis with palm trees, clouds and shooting stars!' and in 1967 it became the Fairmont.

NEW HIBERNIA BANK BUILDING, NEW ORLEANS, LA.

289

HOTEL DE SOTO — NEW ORLEANS, LOUISIANA

AN AFFILIATED NATIONAL HOTEL

290

Cotton Exchange, New Orleans, La.

291

Hotel Grunewald, New Orleans, La.

292

293

NEW YORK, New York
293–301
These nine city landscapes, printed at the turn of the century, are lithographed and contain up to eight flat colour transfers. Sometimes details and tints were added by manual alleatory dot screenings.

294

295

296

297

298

299

116

300

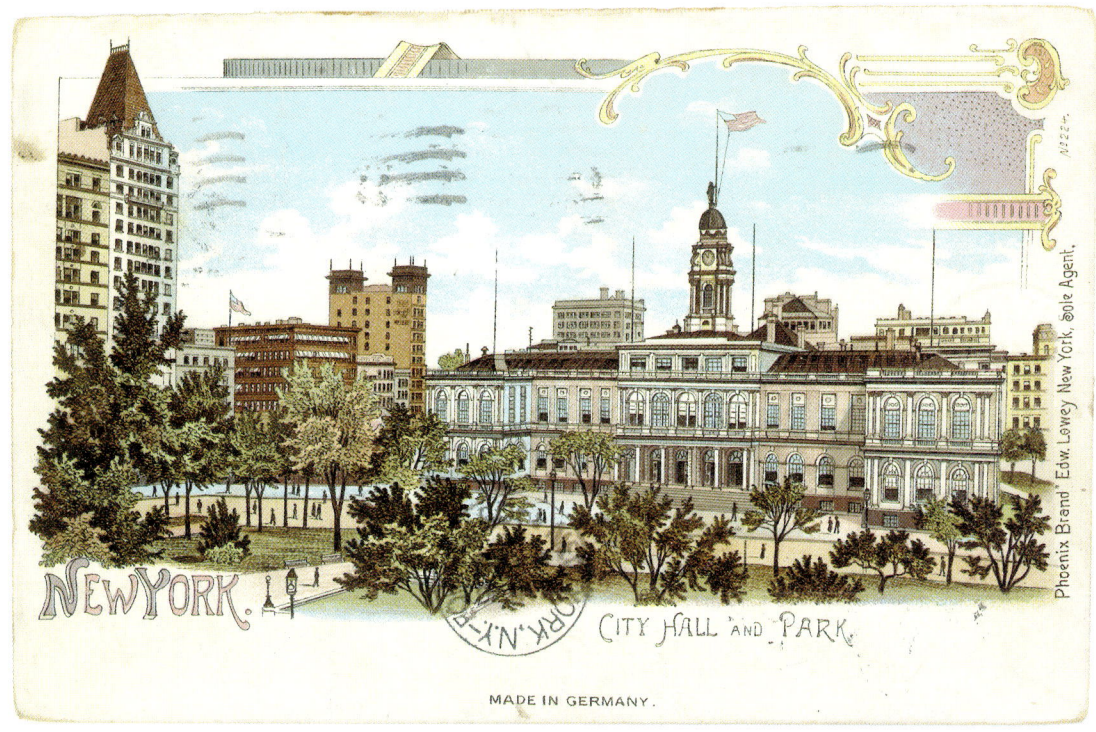

301

302

302 NEW YORK UNIVERSITY, HALL OF FAME, New York City, New York

303 ST LUKE'S HOSPITAL, New York City, New York

304 GENERAL U.S. GRANT'S TOMB, New York City, New York
1897, architect J.H. Duncan. This mausoleum was erected by public subscription to honour the memory of Ulysses S. Grant, 18th president of United States and chief of the Union army during the Civil War. The monument was inspired by the Halicarnasse Mausoleum.

303

304

City Hall, New York,

305

U.S. Series 111/4 Entrance to Brooklyn Bridge, N.Y.

306

307

305–307
CITY HALL, New York City, New York
1811, the competition was won by French architects J. Mangin and S. McComb. An elegant Renaissance Georgian style building (later considered Italianate). Heavy restoration was conducted in 1954. In the sidewalk in front of City Hall is a tablet marking 'the first shovelful of dirt' inaugurating the construction of the New York City Subway on 24 March 1900. The first subway was opened four years later with entrances designed by Heins & La Farge.

308

309

308–309
Two vintage views of the financial district of New York. The Singer Tower that went down in 1968, and that was capable of resisting a 350 ton wind pressure, is clearly visible.

The second postcard view is probably taken from the Woolworth Building.

310

311

312

310–312
SINGER TOWER, New York City, New York 1908, architect E. Flagg. This Beaux Arts style construction was the tallest building in the world for 18 months (612 feet, 47 storeys) until the Metropolitan Life Tower was built. The Singer Building is today the highest building ever demolished (1968). The first Singer Building on Broadway, constructed by the same architect in 1902–04, is intact.

313

313 METROPOLITAN OPERA HOUSE, New York City, New York
Built in 1893, it was closed in 1963 before being transferred to the Lincoln Center in 1966.

314 POLICE HEADQUARTERS, New York City, New York
1909, architect Hoppin & Koen. A 'Barocco' type building, 310 feet long, that has housed 9,500 policeman. It was converted into cooperative apartments in 1973.

315 CRIMINAL COURT BUILDING, New York City, New York
1863–72, called the infamous Tweed Courthouse because of corruption. It is now a designated landmark.

316–318 TRINITY BUILDING (308 feet) and US REALTY BUILDING, New York City, New York
1905 and 1907, architect Francis Kimball. Early twentieth century skyscrapers in a 'modified' Gothic style. A catwalk bridge connects the two buildings. The steel frame was erected in 63 days.

314

315

316

317

318

123

319–326

THE 'EL', New York City, New York

It is difficult to imagine today the number of miles of elevated roads that obstructed downtown New York. The noise was unbearable and the streets were congested up to the second, and sometimes, the third floor. Here are 'El' railways running along important avenues.

319

320

321

322

323

324

325

326

126

327

327 FLAT IRON BUILDING, New York City, New York
1901–03, Chicago architect D.H. Burnham, 21 storeys, 290 feet, six elevators. Flat Iron was the nickname given to the Fuller Building. It was the first building to have a steel framework which was hidden by a French Renaissance facade so as not to frighten the owners. This very popular building is considered to be one of the oldest skyscrapers of New York.

328

329

328–329
BATTERY PARK and LOWER MANHATTAN at the turn of the century and in 1925–30.

330

330–332
WHITEHALL BUILDING, New York City, New York
Large office building facing Battery Park and covering 21 city lots. The 1903 building is 20 storeys (254 feet) high and the new 1911 addition rises to 32 storeys (416 feet).

331

332

333

334

335

336

333–336 TWIN HUDSON TERMINAL, New York City, New York

Office room for 20,000 people, 22 storeys, 375 feet, 18,150,000 cubic feet, 39 elevators. The building is resting on a cofferdam 400 x 178 and 75 to 98 feet deep. It was razed to make way for the 110-storey World Trade Center. Underneath was the terminal of the Hudson and Manhattan tubes entering from Jersey City called 'the Path' which is today located about 100 yards west.

337 NEW YORK LIFE INSURANCE CO., New York City, New York

1926–28, architect Cass Gilbert. The company's home was once on Broadway (1870, architect G. Thomas, enlarged in 1896 by McKim, Mead & White). Today it is on the site of the old Madison Garden – 650 feet, 21,000,000 cubic feet, with 36 elevators for a potential population of 10,000.

338 STANDARD OIL BUILDING, New York City, New York

1922–26, architect Carrère & Hastings with Shreve, Lamb & Blake, 507 feet. On a stepped pyramid stands a colossal aluminium tripod concealing the chimney. Exxon has since moved to the Rockefeller Center

339 NEW YORK STOCK EXCHANGE, New York City, New York

1900–03, architect G. Post. The Stock Exchange has been on this site since 1865. At the entry a tree marks the 17 May 1792 gathering of 24 brokers to lobby for an official place to work. In 1923 architect Trowbridge & Livingstone added the 22-storey annexe.

337

338

339

340

340 COMMODORE VANDERBILT'S GRAND CENTRAL STATION

The 1871 Second Empire building was remodelled and enlarged in 1899. The station depicted in the postcard was torn down to give way to the present Grand Central Terminal designed by C. Gilbert. The acquisition of the rights to the underground tracks in 1903 made the new building necessary.

341–342 GRAND CENTRAL TERMINAL

1919, architects Reed & Stem and Westmore & Warren. In 1903 a design competition was held for a new terminal. Completed in 1913 and finally finished in 1919, the whole network was electrified in 1902. The grand concourse, with waiting rooms, shopping and other facilities, has since been a popular rendezvous. The tracks run on two levels further down.

341

342

132

343

344

345

343–345
PENNSYLVANIA STATION
1906–10, architect McKim, Mead and White. An imposing building with spectacular steel and glass structures (in fact it was supposed to be a replica of the Roman Caracalla Baths). The station fell victim to the real estate logic in 1963. It should have been worshipped as a civic masterpiece.

346

347

346 NEW YORK CENTRAL BUILDING, New York City, New York
1929, architect Warren & Wetmore. This building was possible because of electric traction since the open railroad ran underneath it. Characteristic are its three-storey columns hundreds of feet above the ground. Today it is called the Helmsley Building.

347 PARAMOUNT BUILDING, New York City, New York
1926–27, architect Rapp & Rapp, 35 storeys, 458 feet. Adolph Zukor, president of Paramount Pictures had the Paramount Building constructed to house offices and a 4,000 seat theatre. Once it was an hotel, today it is an office building.

348

349

348 LINCOLN BUILDING, New York City, New York

1929–30, architect Co J.E. Carpenter, 53 storeys. The upper part of the tower is Neo-Gothic but the building is an Art Deco structure with tiers.

In the center of the lobby is a miniature replica of D.C. French bronze sculpture displayed at Washington's Lincoln Memorial.

349 EQUITABLE BUILDING, New York City, New York

1915, architect E.R. Graham. The Equitable Building occupies four city blocks and a rentable floor space of 1,200,000 square feet rising 38 storeys.

350 OLD POST OFFICE, New York City, New York

1869–78, architect supervisor A.B. Mullett. There were no first and second prizes granted for the architect competition, instead the 15 best designs were assembled in an eclectic Neo-Renaissance monument under a supervisory committee of eight architects. It was torn down in 1938–39.

351 GILLENDER BUILDING, New York City, New York

1897, 540 feet. It was demolished to give way to the Banker's Trust Co. Building.

350

351

352

353

354

352–353
The New York City and the Brooklyn Manhattan bridges approaches. None of them are accurate. The architect was influenced by the Porte St Denis arch in Paris and the colonnade is similar in effect to that of St Peter's in Rome (that was what was officially said).

354 SIEGEL-COOPER & COMPANY STORE, New York City, New York
1986, architect DeLemos & Cordes. Henry Siegel arrived from Chicago whereupon the store was set up in five months! Six storeys are topped by a tower. The opening was attended by 150,000 people.

355

356

357

358

355–358
CITY INVESTING BUILDING, New York City, New York
This 34-storey, 486 feet structure could accommodate 6,000 tenants. The ornate eclectic building was torn down with its neighbour, the Singer Tower, in 1968 to give way to the 1 Liberty Plaza Building completed in 1974.

359–361

TIMES BUILDING, New York City, New York

1903–05, architect Eidlitz & McKenzie, 25 storeys. The building was owned by the New York Times until 1961 but was too small for their needs. The Times vacated the premises in 1913. Before the newspaper was there, Times Square was called Long Acre Square. For years it has been just an outdoor piece of advertising.

359

360

361

362 **ELLIS ISLAND Administration Building, New York**

1892, architect Boring & Tilton. A small island (11 hectares) in the bay of New York that became the waiting room of the Promised Land. More than 12 million immigrants landed here between 1892 and 1954 (between 1903 and 1914, there were 2,000 people per day!), 98 percent of whom were accepted in America.

363 **CASTLE CLINTON NATIONAL MONUMENT**

Once West Battery was an island. In 1815 it became Castle Clinton and in 1824, Castle Garden with a 6,000 seat opera hall. In 1855 it was the main immigrant landing station. By 1889, eight million immigrants had landed here. The place was no longer an island as the ditches were filled in. Then came the very popular New York Aquarium, 1896, architect McKim, Mead & White (entrance was free!) that moved in 1902 to Coney Island. The fort was restored and is today a designated landmark.

364 **AQUARIUM**

This was the second largest aquarium in the world. On the right is downtown New York's fireboat station that closed not so long ago.

365

366

367

368

369

370

365–366
MUNICIPAL BUILDING, New York City, New York
1907–16, architect W.M. Kendall of McKim, Mead & White, 580 feet, 34 storeys. The design was the result of a competition, it is the architect's first skyscraper. It is said that the building inspired the grand tower of the University of Moscow. The foundations are made of 116 pneumatic caissons sunk 260 feet under street level and 230 feet under the nearby water level, a very complicated task. Today it houses the Museum of the City of New York.

367–368
CHAMBERS OF COMMERCE, New York City, New York
1901–02, architect James Backer. The Chambers of Commerce were established in 1768 (after Marseilles in France and the Island of Jersey). In 1924 the three marble figure groups were removed because of decomposition. The building, restored in 1991, has been a landmark since 1966.

369–370
PARK ROW BUILDING, New York City, New York
1899, architect Robert Robertson, 29 storeys. This was once the tallest building in the world. Its twin cupolas added interest to the growing skyline. The reception hall and the lobby with its semi-circular elevators are outstanding. It is built entirely of limestone.

371

372

371 NEW YORK COUNTY COURTHOUSE, New York City, New York

1912, architect G. Lowell won the competition. A hexagonal building with an enormous Corinthian portico.

372 The creative design of the postcard artist suggests an interesting version of the new courthouse, or was it a project?

373 CITY HALL, Borough of the Bronx, New York

373

374

375

374 NATIONAL CITY BANK OF NEW YORK, New York City, New York
This 'double-deck Roman revival' was demolished in 1895 to make way for the Sperry & Hutchinson Building, housing the company that introduced trading stamps.

375 Fireboat 'New Yorker' at the Battery Landing, New York City, New York

376 THE PENNSYLVANIA TUNNEL runs under the Hudson River, 60 feet below the surface. At first the trains were drawn by electric motors, the change being made at the Manhattan Transfer just east of Newark, New Jersey.

377

378

379

BRIDGES TO MANHATTAN
Twenty nine bridges link the island of Manhattan to the other boroughs.

377–380
BROOKLYN BRIDGE
Erected between 1870 and 1883, it was opened to the public on 25 May 1883. The bridge was designed and built by engineers John Roebling and his son, Colonel W. Roebling, and supervised by Colonel Roebling's wife after their deaths.

It was the first suspension bridge with steel cables. The two cable towers measure 272 feet from water level. The main span is 1,600 feet with two routes, two railway tracks and a very spectacular pedestrian passage. The bridge approach is 1,562 feet and the total length is 6,357 feet.

Huge caissons (four tennis courts in size each) were sunk down to bedrock. Brooklyn Bridge was the first bridge lit by electricity but is, above all, the technological ancestor of all the great steel cable suspension bridges.

381 MANHATTAN BRIDGE
1901–09, chief engineer C. Ingersoll and architects Carrère & Hastings, L. Morsieff and G. Lindenthal. This bridge was the fourth to span over the East River (eight railway tracks at different levels, four lanes of motor vehicle traffic and subway lines). Steel towers are 336 feet high resting on masonry pedestals. The total length is 8,655 feet.

382–384 WILLIAMSBURG BRIDGE
1903, engineer L. Buck. The caissons were sunk 110 feet below water level. Total length: 7,200 feet, height: 135 feet clear, river span: 1,600 feet.

381

382

383

C.V. 119—WILLIAMSBURG BRIDGE, N.Y. CITY.

384

QUEENSBORO BRIDGE AND BLACKWELL'S ISLAND, NEW YORK CITY.

385

385–386

QUEENSBORO BRIDGE

1893–1909, architect H. Hornbostel and engineer G. Lindenthal. What makes this double deck bridge interesting is the architectural presence in the handering of the decoration of the steel towers. It is the only cantilever bridge in New York (regarded very doubtfully because the Quebec Bridge had collapsed). Total length: 7,636 feet.

QUEENSBOROUGH BRIDGE AND NEW YORK HOSPITAL, NEW YORK CITY

386

387

388

389

390

391

392

393

387 GRAYBAR BUILDING, New York City, New York
1927, architect Sloan and Robertson, 30 storeys. This was once the largest office building in the world and houses 12,000 employees.

388 SIXTY WALL STREET, 362 feet
TRUST CO. OF AMERICA, 327 feet, erected in 1907

389 A free interpretation of the WORLD BUILDING on Park Row with a spectacular rendering of the underground terminal. The World Building was demolished in the early 1950s to make way for the Brooklyn Bridge approaches (1890, architect G.B. Post, 26 storeys).

390 THE 500 FIFTH AVENUE BUILDING, New York City, New York
A 58-storey building overlooking the New York principal public library and Bryant's Park.

391–392 TWIN HUDSON TERMINAL
Two views of the imposing Hudson Terminals seen from the east and from the west. It no longer exists.

393 THE FLAT IRON BUILDING
A view that seems to belong to the 1920s.

394

394 NEW YORK PUBLIC LIBRARY, New York City, New York
1897–1911, architect Carrère & Hastings. The building was erected on the site of the Croton Reservoir. It is considered to be the best example of Beaux Arts architecture although no such building was ever built in France. The library housed more than two million books.

395 GENERAL POST OFFICE, New York City, New York
1910–12, architect McKim, Mead & White. It was built over railroad tracks leading to Pennsylvania Station. Due to the 377 foot long Corinthian colonnade, there is no visible entrance (to be found behind the eleventh bay).

396 US CUSTOM HOUSE, New York City, New York
1899–1907, architect Cass Gilbert, Beaux Arts style. On this spot, formerly occupied by Fort Amsterdam, stood the Merchant Exchange.
1836–42, architect I. Rogers on the site of an earlier one. It became the Custom House and was acquired by the First National City Bank in 1899. Today it is a designated landmark and houses the Museum of the American Indians.

395

396

397

397–399

THREE PLACES OF ENTERTAINMENT

The Churchill's Cabaret, once on Broadway and the famous Hippodrome where in 1871 P.T. Barnum opened what was later to be the first Madison Square Garden. The second Madison Square Garden was opened in 1870 (architect S. White), a three million dollar construction with a Maure tower souvenir from Seville's Giralda. Madison Square Garden was finally rebuilt at West 50th Street and 8th Avenue on the site of Pennsylvania Station. Dismantled in 1963–66, Madison Square Garden is an never ending story.

398

399

400

400 TUDOR CITY (on the left) and EAST RIVER, New York City, New York

Tudor City was constructed between 1925 and 1928 with 12 buildings and 3,000 apartments. The plants and factories were razed to allow for the construction of the United Nations Headquarters in 1952.

401

402

401–402
WOOLWORTH BUILDING, New York City, New York

1910–13, architect Cass Gilbert, 60 storeys, 792 feet, 3,000 offices occupied by 12,000 people. 'The Cathedral of Commerce' opened in 1913 when President Wilson pressed a button in the White House to illuminate the building. It was the tallest building until the completion of the Chrysler Building in 1930.

Built in a flamboyant Gothic revival style, it was influenced by the Houses of Parliament in London. The foundations were made of caissons 19 feet in diameter sunk to bedrock, 110 to 130 feet below the ground. The power plant generates sufficient electrical energy to supply the needs of a city population of 50,000.

403 TRINITY CHURCH, New York City, New York
1841–46, architect R. Upjohn. The parish is supposed to be the richest in the world, owning land in lower Manhattan. In 1694 there was already a church on the spot, destroyed by the great fire in 1776. This is the third construction. The steeple is 280 feet high, a brownstone construction that was the tallest until 1892. The centre building is the former American Surety Building.

404 St PAUL'S CHAPEL, New York City, New York
1766, architect T. McBean. The only church in Manhattan erected before Independence Day. It is a national historic landmark.

405 St PATRICK'S CATHEDRAL
1879, architect J. Penwick. Neo-Gothic church seating 2,500 parishioners, the largest Roman Catholic church in America. The spires were added between 1885 and 1888.

406 CORTLAND STREET, New York City, New York
Although several historic buildings can be recognised, the postcard focuses on the El station. The legend (or is it no legend?) says the stations were constructed with Swiss carpenters, hence the Swiss chalet with low-pitched roofs.

407 90 WEST STREET BUILDING, New York City, New York
1905, architect Cass Gilbert, a 22 storeys gothic revival. The upper part of the building is floodlit at dusk.

408–409
METROPOLITAN LIFE BUILDING, New York City, New York
1893, architect N. Le Brun & Sons. Up to 1909 it was the world's highest tower, 700 feet, 51 storeys. It was modelled after the St Marco tower in Venice. The clocks are 26.5 feet in diameter and the minute hand measures 17 feet.

In 1962, during a period when it was fashionable to strip buildings to give them a modernistic look, the tower and the adjacent company building lost much of their original ornamentation.

406

407

408

409

157

410

411

412

413

414

415

410–411
BARCLAY-VESEY BUILDING, New York City, New York

1923–26, architects J. Walker, McKenzie, Voorhees and Gmelin, 32 storeys. An Art Deco building that is known as the New York Telephone Building.

412–413
A north view and a south view of the 1929 Grand Central Building (40 storeys, 567 feet since 1981) before the erection of the PAN AM BUILDING (MET LIFE since 1981).

414–415
STATUE OF LIBERTY on LIBERTY ISLAND (formerly Bedloe's Island)

The Statue of Liberty was designed by the French sculptor, August Bartholdi, and presented to the United States by the French in 1884. Gustave Eiffel was in charge of the general structure.

The huge Doric pedestal (architect M M. Hunt), which was made of armed concrete and granite, supports the 80 ton sculpture. The statue measures 152 feet and stands on a 155 feet pedestal. The statue and its museum were remodelled in 1986.

416

HOTELS IN NEW YORK

The hotels, as we know them today, are an American invention that started in the 1830s, but the grand luxury hotel had its origin in the 1890s. They became the venue for not only social gatherings but also for business and political meetings – nowhere else could two or three thousand people gather. While life was being lived to the hilt in one part of the hotel, other rooms were being used as single places of trading.

416 HOTEL PENNSYLVANIA
The hotel has 2,200 rooms facing Pennsylvania Station.

417–425
Hotel NEW YORKER
Hotel KNICKERBOCKER
Hotel SAVOY-PLAZA and Hotel NETHERLANDS
Hotel DIXIE
Hotel CENTURY
Hotel WELLINGTON
Hotel VANDERBILT
Hotel SAVOY-PLAZA
Hotel BILTMORE

(Following pages)

426–429
Hotel ST REGIS
Hotel PLYMOUTH
MANHATTAN Hotel. Demolished in 1964
ANSONIA BROADWAY

430–433
Hotel MARTHA WASHINGTON
Hotel BILTMORE
Hotel CHESTERFIELD
AMBASSADOR Hotel

MANHATTAN'S LARGEST HOTEL

417

HOTEL KNICKERBOCKER - NEW YORK CITY

418

419

420

Hotel Century
111 West 46th Street
New York City

421

422

The VANDERBILT Hotel, New York
Park Avenue at Thirty Fourth Street

423

THE SAVOY-PLAZA

424

425

2052—Hotel St. Regis, 5th Ave. and 55th St., New York.
Copyright by Irving Underhill.

426

HOTEL PLYMOUTH
FORTY-NINTH STREET . JUST EAST OF BROADWAY
Adjacent to RADIO CITY New York 19, N. Y.

427

Manhattan Hotel, New York City.

428

THE "ANSONIA" BROADWAY, 73RD AND 74TH STS., NEW YORK

429

430

431

432

433

434

435

436

437

438

439

440

441

442

443

(From previous pages)
   434–437
      Hotel WARWICK
      Hotel DELMONICO
      The ROOSEVELT Hotel
      Hotel SHELTON

   438–441
      Hotel GOVERNOR CLINTON
      Hotel THE LANGWELL
      Hotel TIMES SQUARE
      WILLIAM SLOANE HOUSE – YMCA

442   NEW PLAZA HOTEL
      1888, architect J. Hardenbergh, 800 rooms, 19 storeys, 252 feet. It was inspired by the French Renaissance chateaus. Fatuous settings were installed and heavy restoration was completed by Donald Trump.

443   THE MARTINIQUE HOTEL
      1890, architect H. Hardenbergh. A French Renaissance, 16-storey hotel with 600 rooms. In the 1950s it was one of the few hotels to still offer rooms without baths. The ground rooms were converted to stores and in 1973 it became a short-term shelter for homeless families.

444

445

444 HOTEL McALPIN
1912, architect F.M. Andrews, 25 storeys and three under the ground floor. It was once the largest hotel in New York with 1,620 rooms, all with outside views. Some floors were reserved for women, others for men and even night workers had their own floor where silence was a must during the day! It housed a magnificent 'Marine Grill' in the now demolished basement. The hotel was closed in 1992.

445 ST REGIS HOTEL
1901–04, architect Trowbridge & Livingstone, 18 storeys, 270 feet. The St Regis belongs to the opulent tradition of the mansard-roofed hotels visible in Europe. This hotel is part of the Sheraton network and is sometimes called 'Baroque Hollywood', but it is a classic French Beaux Arts building.

446

447

448

449

450

451

452

453

(From previous pages)

446–447
WALDORF-ASTORIA HOTEL, New York City, New York
1929–31, architect Schultze & Weaver, 47 storeys, 628 feet, 500 rooms. This was once the greatest hotel in the world with its twin 47-storey towers that house suites. The ballroom that can be converted into a theatre is on the third floor. There is a train depot in the basement linked to Grand Central Terminal.

448–449
WALDORF-ASTORIA HOTEL, New York, New York
Architects John Jacob (13 storeys) and H. Hardenbergh (16 storeys). William Waldorf Astor opened his hotel in 1893 and his cousin opened the Astoria 'next door' in 1897. It was demolished in 1929 to give way to the Empire State Building.

450–451
PENNSYLVANIA HOTEL, New York City, New York
Opposite Pennsylvania Railway Terminal, the hotel has 2,200 rooms and 25 storeys with three underground. It is operated by Hotels Statler (Boston, Buffalo, Cleveland, Detroit, St Louis).

450–453
KNICKERBOCKER HOTEL, New York City, New York
1902, architect Marvin & Davis with Bruce Price. The hotel was commissioned by Colonel John Astor IV and is the last of the hotels with mansard roofs on Times Square. In 1920, Vincent Astor, who inherited the Astor properties when his father went down on the Titanic, called in the architect C. Platt to convert the building to offices. It is a perfect Beaux Arts cake.

454

455

456

457

458

454 BELMONT PLAZA, New York City, New York
This hotel has 800 outside rooms.

455–456
HOTEL ST GEORGE, Brooklyn, New York
1885, architect A. Hatfield. In 1929 it was the largest hotel in New York boasting an immense ballroom, an original saltwater pool and low prices. Major renovation was undertaken in the mid 1970s.

457 HOTEL PENNSYLVANIA, New York City, New York
A very delicate engraved postcard.

458 HOTEL ASTOR, New York City, New York
1836, architect I. Rogers. This Beaux Arts building was a replica of the Tremont House in Boston. Partly demolished in 1913, the remaining part was demolished in 1926. It has been replaced by an office building.

171

HOTEL THERESA,
SEVENTH AVENUE, 124th to 125th STREETS,
NEW YORK.
Telephone Monument 1700   R. P. Leube, Manager

459

Hotel Commonwealth, New York City.

460

Hotel Commodore, New York City.
Grand Central Terminal, 42nd Street, New York City.

461

Biltmore Hotel.
Madison Ave., 43rd to 44th St.
New York City.

462

459 HOTEL THERESA
There are 300 outside rooms and a restaurant at the top of the building.

460 HOTEL COMMONWEALTH
This was the first hotel to be erected in conformity with the new building law. It is 400 feet high with 2,500 rooms in 28 storeys. Operated by the people on a profit-sharing plan, 'shares of $100 each will be held by the public'.

461 HOTEL COMMODORE
1917, architect Warren & Wetmore, 26 storeys. Today the facade is covered by bronze-tone glass sheeting. The building is now the 2,000-room Grand Hyatt Hotel with a ballroom and banquet hall for 3,000 people.

462 BILTMORE HOTEL
1912–13, architect Warren & Wetmore, 26 storeys, 1,000 rooms. Today it is called the New Yorker and is owned by the Reverend Sun Myung Moon.

463

464

463–464
CHRYSLER BUILDING, New York City, New York

1928–30, architect William Van Alen, 77 storeys, 1,046 feet. For two years it was the highest building in the world till the completion of the Empire State Building. It houses 15,000 tenants and employees.

The top of the tower is made out of an alloy of nickel and steel – an original material in 1930. Completely ignoring the architect's opinion, Reynolds, the promoter, insisted on a silver top. (Reynolds was the promoter and designer of Dreamland on Coney Island, the 'white pleasure ground'). The facade is decorated with giant radiator caps, genuine wheel disks as well as brick motifs representing Chrysler automobiles.

The building is an Art Deco masterpiece and has been a designated landmark since 1978.

465

466

465–466

ROCKEFELLER CENTER, New York City, New York

In the very heart of Manhattan, the Art Deco Rockefeller Center numbers 21 buildings and skyscrapers in all. Between 1931 and 1940, 14 skyscrapers were built providing work for 225,000 workers during the Depression years.

On the site are 27 radio and television studios, auditoriums (one seating 5,882 people), theatres, hotels and 40 restaurants. There are also buildings such as the RCA Building (1931–33), 70 storeys, 855 feet (today the General Electric Building); the British Empire Building facing la Maison Française; Radio City Music Hall (1932); Equitable Center Tower; the 1903 Lyceum Theatre; the McGraw Hill Building; the Exxon Building (752 feet) and so on.

The architect Raymond Hood directed a team of architects who inaugurated 'vertical town-planning'. The center became a designated landmark in 1985.

175

467

467 The Cunard's mammoth 83,673 ton 'Queen Elizabeth' and the New York skyline. The length of the ship is almost equal to the height of the 1,031 foot Empire State Building.

468 The triumph of Art Deco architecture – the Empire State Building, the RCA Building in Rockefeller Center and the Chrysler Building.

469 The Lower Manhattan skyline by night. At the centre is the City Bank Farmers Trust, on the left is the Bank of Manhattan, and on the right is the Cities Service Building.

468

469

470

470 CHANIN BUILDING, New York City, New York
1929, architect Sloan & Robertson, 56 storeys, 21 elevators. The first skyscraper in the vicinity of Grand Central Terminal. At first it housed the office of Irwin Chanin, a real estate agent. It is a beautiful example of Art Deco architecture.

(Following page)

471 IRVING TRUST COMPANY BUILDING, New York City, New York
1932, architect Voorhees, Gmelin & Walker, 52 storeys. This massive limestone pile of Art Deco is now the Bank of New York Building.

472 FEDERAL COURT AND SUPREME COURT BUILDINGS, New York City, New York
Architect J.B. Lord. On the right is a 37-story structure, 579 feet, built in 1936. On the left is the new Supreme Court Building which was completed in 1935.

473 BANK OF MANHATTAN, New York City, New York
1929, architect H. Severance & Y. Matsui, 69 storeys. First a quasi-public utility known as the Manhattan Company, today it is the Chase Manhattan Bank. A curious detail: the building was topped with a green pyramid that is not brass.

474 CITY BANK FARMERS TRUST CO., New York City, New York
1931, architect Cross & Cross, 750 feet high. This is a 59-storey lime Art Deco shaft constructed on an irregular plot of land.

471

472

473

474

475

476

477

478

479

(From previous page)

475 THE FINANCIAL CENTRE, New York City, New York
The Federal Reserve Bank, Cities Service, Bank of Manhattan, City Bank and the Farmers Trust Company Building can be seen in this view.

476 PARK AVENUE looking south, New York City, New York
Underneath run the tracks of the New York Central Railroad concealed by park spaces. On the left is the Ritz Tower apartment building – 1925–26, architect E. Roth, 380 feet, 41 storeys.

477 FIFTH AVENUE and 42ND STREET, New York City, New York
A busy corner of the New York Public library.

478 WALL STREET, New York City, New York
leading to the US Sub-Treasury

479–483
EMPIRE STATE BUILDING, New York City, New York
1929–31, architect William Lamb, Schreve & Harmon Associates, 102 storeys, 73 elevators, 1,250 feet from the sidewalk to what was to be the mooring mast for dirigibles. Observatories are open on the 86th and 102nd floors. The 30 upper floors are lit from dusk until the middle of the night. The building houses 15,000 people.

The Empire State Building hit a record, rising four stories per week. It was completed in less than two years and became a designated landmark in 1981.

480

481

482

483

181

484

485

486

487

488

489

484–485   THE FINANCIAL DISTRICT, New York City, New York
The Federal Reserve Bank is in the foreground. Also visible is the Cities Service, the Bank of Manhattan, City Bank and the Farmers Trust Company's buildings.

486–487   PARAMOUNT and TIMES SQUARE BUILDINGS, New York City, New York
The Paramount Theater was one of the leading motion picture palaces. On the right is the Hotel Astor and in the near distance, the New York Times Building.

488   A midtown view showing the Chrysler, Daily News, Chanin, Lincoln and Lefcourt Buildings. Brooklyn is in the far distance.

489   Downtown skyline from the Staten Island Ferry.
On the right is the Governor's Island Ferry Terminal. 1906–07, architect Walker & Morris. The ornaments are made of steel on a steel structure. The terminal now serves the United States Coast Guard quartered at Governor's Island.

490

491

492

493

494

490   CITY HALL, Oakland, California

491   THE HOFMANN BUILDING, Ottumwa, Iowa

492   HOTEL FONTENELLE, Omaha, Nebraska

493   W.O.W. BUILDING, Omaha, Nebraska

494   BURLINGTON STATION, Omaha, Nebraska

495

496

495 UNION BUILDING, San Diego, California

496 HOTEL CARLTON, Portland, Oregon

497 MINOT'S LIGHT, Massachusetts
The famous New England Lighthouse located one and a half miles offshore. Built in 1860, 88 feet high, the lower half is solid all the way through. Five years were needed to construct it.

498 RACINE REEF LIGHTHOUSE, Wisconsin
Located three miles offshore on Lake Michigan.

499–500
Giant Sahuaro Cactus in Arizona

MINOT'S LIGHT, MASSACHUSETTS BAY 50

497

2189 Racine Reef Lighthouse, Three Miles from Shore

Racine, Wisconsin

498

D-17 World's Largest Sahuaro Cactus

499

D-60 "Watermelon Tree," Freak Sahuaro, Giant Cactus

500

29. MANUFACTURERS' CLUB, PHILADELPHIA, PA.

501

Hotel Lorraine, On the Lincoln Highway, Broad St. at Fairmount Ave., Philadelphia, Pa.

502

114 ELVERSON BUILDING AT NIGHT.
HOME OF THE PHILA. INQUIRER, PHILADELPHIA, PA.

503

38. HOTEL ADELPHIA, PHILADELPHIA, PA.

504

505

506

507

PHILADELPHIA, Pennsylvania

501 MANUFACTURER'S CLUB

502 HOTEL LORRAINE

503 ELVERSON BUILDING

504 HOTEL ADELPHIA

505 BELLEVUE-STRATFORD HOTEL
The lobby was on the second floor, the ground floor being used for shops. The first hotel to have air conditioning and zenithal lighting. A curious story: a Foreign Legion convention brought legionnaire's disease to the hotel 25 years ago, and 34 people died.

506 WIDENER BUILDING

507 BETZ BUILDING

508

509

510

PHILADELPHIA, Pennsylvania

- 508 ARCADE BUILDING
- 509 BROAD STREET STATION
  1982, architect Wilson Bros & Co.
- 510 PHILADELPHIA & READING TERMINAL
  Today the station houses the Farmers' Market and more recently the Hard Rock Café.
- 511 FAIRMOUNT WATER WORKS
- 512 PHILADELPHIA OPERA HOUSE
- 513 THE WANAMAKER STORE
  1909–10, architect D. Burnham, 12 storeys above ground and three below. The store closed in 1995 and reopened as Strawbridge's. Recently renovated.

1. Fairmount Water Works, Philadelphia   Copyright 1907 by Taylor Art Co.

511

512

185:—The Wanamaker Store, Philadelphia, Pa.

513

514

515

PHILADELPHIA, Pennsylvania

514   OLD WALNUT STREET PRISON, 1774

515   CITY HALL
Designed by J. McArthur Jr. in 1869, but built in 1874–80. This late Second Empire Louvre style building has a 511 feet disproportionate tower with a 37-feet sculpture of William Penn made by Calder, the grandfather of Alexander Calder. There are no steel armatures so the base of the walls is 22 feet thick. The building was finally completed in 1907. The hall itself took 10 years to build and 20 more to be decorated.

516   PENNA RAILROAD SUBURBAN STATION BUILDING
This huge 1935 construction houses a railway station and the United States Post Office. As with other places, the flat roof was built to allow for deliveries by mail plane.

516

517

518

PITTSBURGH, Pennsylvania

517 B & O STATION
518 FORT PITT HOTEL

519

520

521

522

523 HOTEL WEBSTER HALL — Pittsburgh, Pa.

524 T. J. KEENAN BUILDING, PITTSBURGH, PA.

525 PITTSBURGHER HOTEL, PITTSBURGH, PA.

526 Farmer's National Bank, Pittsburg, Pa.

(from previous pages)

PITTSBURGH, Pennsylvania

- 519 THE FRICK BUILDING
- 520 HENRY W. OLIVER BUILDING
  1910, 25 storeys and two underground, 1163 offices.
- 521 ARROT BUILDING
- 522 FIRST NATIONAL BANK BUILDING
- 523 HOTEL WEBSTER HALL
- 524 T.J. KEENAN BUILDING
- 525 PITTSBURGHER HOTEL
- 526 FARMER'S NATIONAL BANK

527

528

529

ARLINGTON MILLS, LAWRENCE, MASS.

530

527–532
There was a time when the importance of an industry could be measured by the size of the site. Industrial plants in Battle Creek, Michigan; Akron, Ohio; Schenectady, New York; Lawrence, Massachusetts and South St. Paul, Michigan.

531

AERIAL VIEW OF ARMOUR & COMPANY, SOUTH ST. PAUL, MINN.

532

197

533

534

ROCHESTER, New York

533–535
    The river Genesee has generated spectacular plants along its banks.

536 THE NEW CLINIC
    This clinic dates back to the time of the cyclone in 1883.

537 EASTMAN KODAK OFFICE BUILDING

SEATTLE, Washington

538 HOTEL FRYE

539 L.C. SMITH BUILDING
    The 42-storey building rests on 1,276 concrete piles driven 50 feet into the earth. Six stores and 600 offices. Houses an observatory and 'The Chinese Room'.

535

536

537

538

539

199

540

541

540 **KALAKALA MOTOR FERRY**
A ferry cruising between Seattle and Bremerton, Washington. Built in 1935 it could carry 2,000 passengers and 110 automobiles. Its five decks and 25 watertight compartments made the structure virtually unsinkable. It measured 276 feet long and cruised at the modest speed of 18 knots (21 miles per hour) which could hardly justify its name as the first streamline ferry.

(Note from the author: I was much surprised to encounter a similar but much smaller Kalakala, but with no room for cars, cruising in the port of Rotterdam, the Netherlands in 1996).

541 OLYMPIC HOTEL, Seattle, Washington

542 PARRY APARTMENTS, Seattle, Washington

542

543

SALT LAKE CITY, Utah

543 HOTEL UTAH

544 THE MORMON TEMPLE
1853–93, architect B. Young & T. Angel. The Mormon church was started in 1830 in the state of New York. The Temple, with its six towers, was completed 40 years after the cornerstone had been laid. The building was 186 feet long by 99 feet wide, the foundation walls were 16 feet thick and 108 feet high with the east tower rising 210 feet.

545 THE PAVILION

544

545

546

547

ST. LOUIS, Missouri

546–547
: **EADS BRIDGE**
  Inaugurated on 4 July 1874, engineer J.B. Eads. The centre arch is 520 feet wide and the two adjacent arches measure 502 feet each. At the time it was the longest bridge in the world except for a steel suspension bridge in Wales built in 1826 which spanned 580 feet. The bridge has two decks, the top one for vehicles and pedestrians, the lower one for the railroad tracks (no longer in use). It became a national historic monument in 1965.

548 THE MASONIC TEMPLE

549
: **MISSOURI ATHLETIC CLUB**
  1916, 11 storeys, large and small dining rooms seating 1,000 in all, and naturally all sport facilities available with 170 sleeping rooms and suites.

550
: **WRIGHT BUILDING**
  1890–91, architect Adler & Sullivan.

551 PIERCE BUILDING

548

549

550

551

552

Miscellaneous

552   KAUFMANN'S 'THE BIG STORE', Pittsburg, Pennsylvania

553   ST. CHARLES HOTEL, New Orleans, Louisiana

554   LAWRENCE HOTEL, Erie, Pennsylvania

555   COURT HOUSE and CITY HALL, Kansas City, Missouri
1936, architect Wight & Wight, 32 storeys high.

556   PETTICOAT LANE which really was a street specialising in lingerie shops, Kansas City, Missouri

557   HOTEL FORT SHELBY, Detroit, Michigan

558   ATLANTA BILTMORE, Atlanta, Georgia

553

554

555

556

557

558

SAN FRANCISCO, California

559–560
    18th April 1906, the earthquake.
    THE CITY HALL and the Great Fire

561 PACIFIC BUILDING

559

560

561

562

563

562 STANDARD OIL BUILDING

563 THE SKYLINE

564 NEW SOUTHERN PACIFIC BUILDING
1917, architect Bliss & Faville. This was the largest office building west of Chicago.

564

565

566

567

568

569

St. Dominic's Church, San Francisco, California after the earthquake April 18, 1906.

570

1777 – KOHL BUILDING, CALIFORNIA AND MONTGOMERY STREETS, SAN FRANCISCO, CALIFORNIA.

571

The Call and Humboldt Bank Building, San Francisco, California.

572

SING FAT CO., INC.
THE FAMOUS ORIENTAL BAZAAR
S.W. CORNER CALIFORNIA ST. AND GRANT AVE.
CHINATOWN.
SAN FRANCISCO CALIFORNIA.
BRANCH: 615 SOUTH BROADWAY,
LOS ANGELES.

(from previous pages)

565 THE PHELAN BUILDING

566 WESTBANK BUILDINGS

567 FLOOD BUILDING

568 CROCKER BUILDING

569 ST. DOMINIC'S CHURCH after the earthquake

570 KOHL BUILDING

571 THE SAN FRANCISCO CALL BUILDING (today the Spreckles)
1897, architect JW & MJ Reid.

572 SING FAT CO
The oriental bazaar on the corner of California Street.

573

573–574
Looking down, and up, the famous California street with its cable cars climbing Nob Hill (or Nabob!).

574

575

576

577

SAN FRANCISCO, California

575 CLIFF HOUSE
Nobody really knows the number of times this amazing structure has burned down partly or totally. Seals and sea-lions can still be observed from the present-day and sadly rather banal restaurant which now stands on its site.

576 UNION FERRY BUILDING AND DEPOT
Before the completion of the bridge more than a million ferry commuters passed through the ferry building every week. Built in 1915, the tower is 240 feet high.

577 PALACE HOTEL
1875, destroyed by fire during the 1906 earthquake and reconstructed in 1909. Now called the Sheraton Palace Hotel.

578

579

SAN FRANCISCO, California

578   Skyscrapers overlooking the bay.

579   Portsmouth Square where Commodore J. Montgomery raised the flag to herald American possession of California, 8 July 1846.

Other buildings worthy of note:

580–582
A court house in Grand Rapids, Michigan; the Mount Tom Summit House in Holyoke, Massachusetts and a C & O Passenger Depot in Newport News, Virginia.

580

581

582

583

584

585

586

587

588

589

590

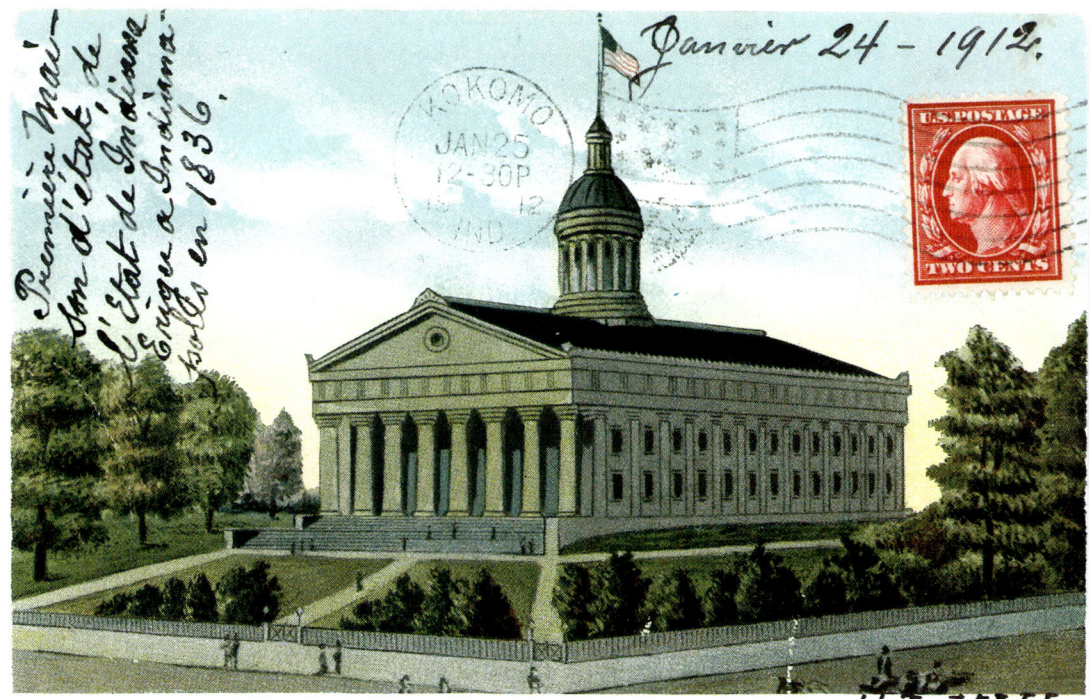

591

592

The are but a few state capitols that are not Neo-Classical. The mould was set and was to continue – the establishment is Neo-Classic. The same type of architecture is to be found in many city halls, courthouses and public buildings.

583–590
    Here are the state capitol buildings of Texas, Georgia, California, Pennsylvania, Rhode Island, Wisconsin, Indiana and Utah.

591   FIRST STATE HOUSE, Indianapolis, Indiana. 1836.

592   THE CAPITOL BUILDING, Washington, DC
The cornerstone was laid by President Washington in 1793 with an original design by W. Thornton. Overlooking the amphitheatre of the River Potomac, the building is 751 feet long and 350 wide. The statue of Freedom on the cast-iron dome towers 307 feet above the Esplanade (architect T. Walter, 1855–64).

The central building was finished in 1797 (architect B. Latrobe) and the extensions were first occupied by Congress in 1857 and 1859. The central building is connected by corridors with the House and Senate wings.

WASHINGTON, DC

593 **LINCOLN MEMORIAL**
Modelled after a classic Greek temple. The monumental marble structure is a memorial to Abraham Lincoln. The walls are surrounded by 36 columns representing each of the 36 states in the Union at the time of Lincoln's death.

594 **LIBRARY OF CONGRESS, 1877**
The inside decorations are superb but have nothing in common with Neo-Classicism.

595 **NEW ARCHIVES BUILDING**

LINCOLN MEMORIAL, WASHINGTON, D. C.
593

Library of Congress, Washington, D. C.
594

M534:—NEW ARCHIVES BUILDING, CONSTITUTION AND PENNSYLVANIA AVENUES, WASHINGTON, D. C.
595

596

597

598

596 TREASURY DEPARTMENT

597 DEPARTMENT OF JUSTICE
The size of the building gives the illusion of bas-relief facades.

598 PENSION OFFICE
1882–85, architect General M. Meigs. This is supposed to be the largest brick building in the world, inspired by the Palazzo Farnese in Rome. The hall is 159 feet long with eight huge columns of 89 feet. The Inauguration Ball was attended by 18,000 people. Nine presidents have inaugurated meeting or balls here. Today it houses the National Museum of Building Arts.

WASHINGTON, DC

599 THE WASHINGTON OLD POST
1899, architect J. Willoughby. This granite building housed the administrative offices of the United States Postal Services. Nicknamed 'the old tooth' it was obsolete for quite a time and was remodelled between 1978–83. Today it is an elegant shopping concourse and houses various offices.

600 MASONIC TEMPLE

601 WASHINGTON COUNTY COURT HOUSE

602 THE AMERICAN RED CROSS
This mansion is dedicated to the memory of the heroic women in the civil war and houses the administrative departments of the American Red Cross.

603 UNITED STATES SUPREME COURT BUILDING
A classic Corinthian design with lofty columns, it faces the Capitol Building.

599

600

601

602

603

604

604 Snow and oranges in California.

605 Cape Horn, the Columbia River: the frontier between the states of Washington and Oregon showing the North Bank Railway Tunnel.

606 St Petersburg, Florida
The sunken gardens.

605

606

NOTES

NOTES

NOTES

Every effort has been made to trace the original source of copyright material contained in this book. The publishers would be pleased to hear from copyright holders to rectify any errors or omissions.
The information and illustrations in this publication have been prepared and supplied by Luc Van Malderen. While all reasonable efforts have been made to ensure accuracy, the publishers do not, under any circumstances, accept responsibility for errors, omissions and representations express or implied.